The Five Points of Free Grace

Shawn Lazar

Longview, TX

Published by Free Grace International
2 Circle Rd
Longview, TX 75602
www.freegrace.in

Shawn Lazar (1978–)

ISBN: 978-1-68543-019-1 (Paperback)
978-1-68543-020-7 (Kindle)

Contents

Introduction

There comes a point in every Christian's life when you begin to realize that not everyone believes the same. Not only are there different denominations, but there can also be different theological beliefs within each denomination. And when you start asking bigger questions about God, Jesus, and how salvation is supposed to work, someone may tell you there are only two camps, *Calvinism* or *Arminianism*, and *you're either in one or the other.*

I remember being introduced to Calvinism in college. I had been a Christian for a little over a year when a fellow student gave me a dot-matrix printout of R. L. Dabney's essay, *The Five Points of Calvinism*. I read it on a long bus ride home during one of Montreal's cold winter evenings. But Dabney's arguments are what chilled me to the bone. Point after point, he presented a picture of God and salvation that I had never heard before and which was starkly different from what I believed. Then again, I was so new to Christianity that I wasn't sure what to believe. I had never heard of Calvinism or of any other school of theology. It was all new to me. But I trusted the friend who gave me the essay, and as far as I could tell, Dabney quoted Scripture, his arguments seemed logical, and his claims fit together. More importantly, no one presented me with an alternative. So, I believed him, and became a Calvinist, but I wasn't happy about it. I gained a theological system, but I lost my joy.

It took several more years of studying theology, growing spiritually, and learning about the Bible before I became convinced that Calvinism is false. (I can tell you the very day I had the breakthrough that made me leave Calvinism—but that's a story for another time.)

But even though I rejected Calvinism, I wasn't Arminian either. For a while, I didn't know what I was. I had no name for it.

Years later I came across the Free Grace position. It was neither Calvinist nor Arminian, but something different, and I believed it was closer to what I saw taught in Scripture.

As you might know, Calvinism and Arminianism are often summarized using flower acronyms. Calvinism is famously represented by TULIP, which stands for:

T— Total depravity
U— Unconditional election
L— Limited atonement
I— Irresistible grace
P— Perseverance/preservation of the saints.

Meanwhile, Arminians have used different acronyms (e.g., ACURA, DAISY, FACTS), but to keep with the botanic theme, ROSES stands for:

R— Radical depravity
O— Overcoming grace
S— Sovereign election
E— Eternal life
S— Singular redemption.

Daniel Weierbach devised a flower acronym for the Free Grace position, namely, LOTUS[1], which I define this way:

L— Liable depravity
O— Occupational election
T— Tiered atonement
U— Undeserved grace
S— Security of the saints.

It's always tricky to fit a theology into an acronym, but I think LOTUS works well. I'll soon explain what each of those points means, but before I do, you should know that Free Grace is a relatively young movement. Yes, the truths we hold are as old as Scripture, and the debate over the role of faith and works in salvation pops up throughout history, but Free Grace has only recently developed as a systematic position. That means while Calvinists and Arminians have been working on their theology for *centuries*, we've only been doing it for *decades*. Consequently, while some doctrines are settled, others are still being worked out.

And like Calvinism and Arminianism, Free Grace isn't monolithic. We don't always agree on the interpretation of every single verse or the answer to every theological question. That means *I don't speak for everyone*. Although I will be writing about "the" Free Grace position, let me clarify this is "my" personal contribution to the tradition. Of the five points in LOTUS, I would say there's strong agreement in Free Grace circles when it comes to *undeserved grace* and the *security of the saints*. If there will be disagreement, it will be in how I develop the first three points. In any case, this booklet is my constructive approach to developing a more Biblical alternative to traditional Calvinist or Arminian soteriology. While I trust that many Free Grace people will agree with me, others will give different answers, and I encourage you to seek those out (see the Bibliography).

I have two goals here—one modest and one ambitious.

My modest goal is to convince you that Free Grace *is a legitimate third option*. Even if I don't convince you that it's true, I hope it will help you realize that you don't have to choose between Calvinism and Arminianism. If Calvinists and Arminians can admit that Free Grace is a legitimate alternative, I will have accomplished an important goal of changing the conversation and raising the profile of Free Grace thought.

Of course, my more ambitious goal is to convince you *these five positions are true*. Even if you don't accept every detail of my arguments, I hope you'll believe my general approach is more faithful to the Bible than either Calvinism or Arminianism.

Who did I write this for? Essentially, I wrote this for my younger self, riding the bus home, reading Dabney, and trying to figure out the mysteries of salvation. I wish I had an essay like this when I was first investigating Calvinism and Arminianism. If you know someone who's struggling with these issues, please share this with them. I wrote it to be simple but not simplistic. There are very few quotations and footnotes. I want as many intelligent people to read this as possible.

My motivation is simple: to be faithful to my Lord Jesus, to His Word, and to benefit His Church. I'm interested in getting to the truth, not winning arguments. If that's your desire, too, and if you have an open mind, let's investigate these issues together.

Endnotes

1. Please see Daniel Weierbach, *LOTUS: A Free Grace Response to TULIP* (2024): www.c4capologetics.com

1
Liable Depravity

The first point in each of the acronyms, whether TULIP, ROSES, or LOTUS, concerns *sin*.

Calvinists believe in what's known as *total depravity*. More importantly, they believe in something called *total inability*. That means sin has so affected us that we can't believe in Jesus *without being regenerated first*. Lorraine Boettner states this clearly in his booklet *The Reformed Faith*:

> "Because of the fall in Adam man is unable of himself to savingly believe the Gospel...Consequently, it takes much more than the Spirit's assistance to bring a sinner to Christ—it takes regeneration by which the Spirit brings a sinner from spiritual death to spiritual life and gives him a new nature."[1]

In Calvinism, regeneration precedes faith. And since you can't choose to regenerate yourself, Calvinists reason that God must decide whom to regenerate and, therefore, who will believe and be saved. In other words, the doctrine of total inability leads to the belief that God predestines specific individuals to salvation—and damns the rest.

Similarly, many Arminians agree that unregenerate people are totally depraved and unable to believe in Jesus. But instead of concluding that people must be regenerated before faith, many Arminians say God sends His prevenient grace to *partially* regenerate people. As Roger Olson explains:

> "The person who receives the full intensity of prevenient grace (i.e., through the proclamation of the Word and the corresponding internal calling of God) is no longer dead in tresspasses and sins. However, such a person is not yet fully regenerated. The bridge between partial regeneration by prevenient grace and full regeneration by the Holy Spirit is *conversion*, which includes repentance and faith."[2]

Therefore, despite some differences, both traditions believe in total depravity and total inability. They have different answers as to how God deals with that problem, but they both agree on the nature of the problem.

By contrast, in the Free Grace view (as I conceive it), sin has affected all of human life to the point that we can't possibly be saved on the basis of our works. However, sin has not robbed us of the ability to believe.

The doctrine of sin is a very big and very difficult topic. I think it has been made all the more difficult by how Calvinists and Arminians have inherited a tangled web of assumptions and traditions sin. Instead of trying to untangle those, let's start from scratch, go back to the Bible, and build our understanding of sin from the ground up.

A. The Nature of Sin

What is sin? Simply put, it's a choice to act contrary to God's commands. For example, John defined sin as *lawlessness*:

> **Everyone who commits sin practices lawlessness; and sin is lawlessness (1 John 3:4).**

God's will is the supreme law of life. In fact, God Himself is the standard of right and wrong (cf. Romans 6:23). Jesus summarized the standard we must meet in this way:

> **"Be perfect, therefore, as your heavenly Father is perfect" (Matthew 5:48).**

That's simple but absolutely terrifying. I've never lived up to it. Have you? The demand for perfection is an accusation against every single part of our life. If you hear the demand clearly, you'll realize you're worse off than you think. Nothing you do measures up to perfection, i.e., to God's glory.

God knows we hate facing truths like that. We will admit to having flaws and making mistakes, but we don't like to admit how deep the sin goes. Knowing that about us, God gave us commands to shine a spotlight on our sins. As Paul explained:

> **What should we say then? Is the law sin? Absolutely not! But I would not have known sin if it were not for the law. For example, I would not have known what it is to covet if the law had not said, Do not covet (Romans 7:7).**

God gave the law to reveal our sin. Paul had personally experienced the law's convicting power. As he says, he had been a covetous person without realizing it. But when he heard the command against wanting what other people had (cf., Exodus 20:17), he realized his guilt. That's what God's commands do: they reveal our many sins (and by extension, our need for a Savior).

God reveals His law in Scripture, but He also writes it on the heart:

> **They show that the work of the law is written on their hearts. Their consciences confirm this. Their competing thoughts either accuse or even excuse them (Romans 2:15).**

The claim that sin means transgressing God's command is confirmed when Paul says that if there's no law to transgress, then there's no sin to commit:

> **And where there is no law, there is no transgression (Romans 4:15b).**

For example, since God hasn't forbidden growing a beard, it's not a sin if you do. No law, no transgression.

The fact that sinning primarily means breaking God's commands is shown in the nature of His judgments. In Romans, Paul is clear that God judges *works*:

> **Because of your hardened and unrepentant heart you are storing up wrath for yourself in the day of wrath, when God's righteous judgment is revealed. *He will repay each one according to his works*: eternal life to those who by persistence in doing good seek glory, honor, and immortality; but wrath and anger to those who are self-seeking and disobey the truth while obeying unrighteousness (Romans 2:5-8, emphasis added).**

In Romans 1:18–2:4, Paul painted a sobering picture of humanity's deep dive into greater and greater depravity. While it might look like

God is overlooking those sins, the gospel revealed that a day of wrath was coming when all those works would be judged and repaid—a judgment from which all who believe in Christ will be saved (cf. Matthew 10:15; John 3:18; 5:22-29; Acts 10:42; 17:31; 24:25; Romans 1:16-17; 5:9).

But sin is not just choosing to do the evil God has forbidden but also failing to do the good He has commanded:

> **So it is sin to know the good and yet not do it (James 4:17).**

Sin is by comission or omission. Either way, sin is the moral choice to disobey God's commands.

B. How You Begin to Sin

The next question is, how do you begin sinning? Here's how James describes it:

> **No one undergoing a trial should say, "I am being tempted by God," since God is not tempted by evil, and he himself doesn't tempt anyone. But each person is tempted when he is drawn away and enticed by his own evil desire. Then after desire has conceived, it gives birth to sin, and when sin is fully grown, it gives birth to death (James 1:14-15).**

Think of it as a five-stage process.

First, sin begins with a *suggestion*. That suggestion to sin doesn't come from God. Maybe it comes from an offer someone makes or through an image that you see, or it may even come from an urge in your own body. But somehow the suggestion that you should commit this or that sin comes to you.

Second, the suggestion must correspond to an *evil desire* that you have. For example, if a drug dealer offered you recreational drugs (falling under the prohibition against drunkenness), and you had previously seen the devastating toll of drug use on your family, you probably wouldn't be tempted by the offer. But if you had been curious about what it felt like to get high, you might have that corresponding desire. If the suggestion to sin corresponds to an evil desire it becomes a *temptation*.

Third, you can either reject the temptation or entertain it. If you entertain it, at that point, you've been drawn away by the desire and have "conceived" the sin in your mind. Your heart is like a womb for sins. It's the place where sin is conceived, grows, and develops in your intentions, plans, and choices to transgress God's command. For example, before deciding to send the flood, God said:

> **When the Lord saw that human wickedness was widespread on the earth and that *every inclination of the human mind* was nothing but evil all the time... (Genesis 6:5, emphasis added).**

Likewise, the Lord taught:

> **For from the heart come evil thoughts, murders, adulteries, sexual immoralities, thefts, false testimonies, slander (Matthew 15:19).**

Where do sins start? In your heart or mind.

Fourth, if you choose to act on that sin, you "give birth" to it in your behavior. Temptation becomes a gory reality.

Fifth, and finally, when that newborn sin is fully grown it produces death—all kinds of different sorts of death, for "the wages of sin is death" (cf. Romans 6:23).

If sin means giving into temptation and breaking God's commands, how many people have sinned?

C. Everyone Sins

The short answer is everyone capable of moral actions. No one who can to live up to perfection does it—except for Jesus.

The Lord knew that everyone sins and used it as a preaching strategy. For example, there's a powerful moment in Christ's ministry when some self-righteous men caught a woman in the act of adultery and dragged her (but not her paramour) through the streets of Jerusalem, put her in front of Jesus, and loudly demanded to know whether He thought she should be stoned, just as the Law demanded. Jesus didn't answer. He stooped down and wrote something in the dirt with His finger. We don't know what He wrote. Some commentators imagine that He wrote the seventh commandment. Whatever it was, the crowd refused to accept His silence and pushed for an answer about what to do with the woman. The Lord finally stood up and said:

> **"The one without sin among you should be the first to throw a stone at her" (John 8:7b).**

Then Jesus stooped back down and went back to writing in the dirt.

Do you remember what happened? The crowd melted away. No one could throw the stone. Significantly, John says the older men left first. Maybe they knew they had dodged stones for years. Eventually, everyone left. Why? Because everyone is a sinner. Jesus knew that. And if we're honest, we should know that, too. In a different context, Jesus put it simply:

> **"Why do you call me good?" Jesus asked him. "No one is good except God alone" (Mark 10:18).**

Now that we know everybody sins, we can examine what the Bible has to say about how sin affects us.

D. Sin Results in Physical Corruption

The first effect of sin is *physical corruption,* or more simply, *physical death*. When God warned Adam and Eve about sin, He warned them about dying from it:

> **"but you must not eat from the tree of the knowledge of good and evil, for *on the day you eat from it, you will certainly die*" (Genesis 2:17, emphasis added).**

Most commentators note that Adam and Eve didn't die the same day they ate the fruit, but only hundreds of years later. So what really happened? Some conclude that Adam and Eve must have died *spiritually* that day. But that's not what the text says. (However, I do believe in spiritual death, as I will shortly explain.) So what did God's warning mean? I think John Walton offers a reasonable explanation:

> "Jeremiah 26:8 uses the same phrase as we have in Genesis 2:17, but it is Jeremiah 26:11 that shows us exactly what the people mean by using that phrase in verse 8. When they say, 'You will surely die,' they are talking about the eventual outcome of the behavior. The sentence will be passed, the doom will be fixed... The resulting paraphrase of Genesis 2:17 then is: 'When you eat of it, you will be sentenced to death and therefore doomed to die.' Consequently, death will be a certainty."[3]

By eating the fruit, Adam and Eve started the process of physical corruption that would end in their physical death. And tragically, for us, their mortality was passed on to their descendants. Physical corruption is inheritable, and we all suffer from it.

Physical corruption figures prominently in Jesus' many healings and in how Paul lamented that he had a "body of sin" (Romans 6:6) or a "body of death" (Romans 7:24) and eagerly awaited "the redemption of our bodies" (Romans 8:23), which Jesus promised to believers (John 11:25-26).

But sin affects more than our bodies.

E. Sin Results in Moral Corruption

The second effect of sin is *moral corruption.* It affects not only our bodies but also our characters. It takes time and effort to develop a sin into a vice or an addiction, and people work at it every day! The more you choose to sin, the easier it will be, and the more corrupt you'll become. As Solomon said:

> **I have discovered that *God made people upright,* but they pursued many schemes (Ecclesiastes 7:29, emphasis added).**

Please note that God creates people upright, not totally depraved. What happens is that people pursue their sinful schemes and corrupt themselves. Read Romans 1–3, and you'll see how the downward spiral into sin begins with people who know God but who refuse to act on the truth they know (2:19-23). That leads to them being given over the sinful desires (2:24), then to disgraceful passions (3:26), then to a corrupt mind (3:28), and then all hell breaks loose as society disintegrates into "envy, murder, quarrels, deceit, and malice" (3:29).

The Bible takes a very sobering view of the sinfulness of man, but Calvinists and Arminians can miss the sinner's *progressive* corruption. People aren't born with a hardened or stony heart. Rather, they become hardened (Zechariah 7:12), calloused (Ephesians 4:18-19; Matthew 13:15), and sear their own consciences (1 Timothy 4:2). They're not born spiritually blind but become blind (John 9:39-41) by choosing to shut their own eyes to the truth (Matthew 13:15; Acts 28:27). People are not born deaf but become deaf (Zechariah 7:11; see Matthew 13:15; Acts 28:27) and refuse to listen (Psalms 81:8-13; Jeremiah 6:16-17). They're not born foolish and unable to understand and respond to the Gospel, but choose to exchange knowledge of God for the foolishness of idols (Romans 1:21-23).

The idea that people are born physically corrupt but morally upright is confirmed by the Biblical teaching that young children are *innocent.*

F. Children Are Innocent

Although we all end up in moral depravity, that's not where we began. Yes, babies cry and scream and hit, but those aren't morally culpable actions. According to Scripture (not to mention common sense), a child needs to meet a minimum level of knowledge before he's capable of genuinely moral actions. For example:

> **For before *the boy knows to reject what is bad and choose what is good,* the land of the two kings you dread will be abandoned (Isaiah 7:16, emphasis added).**

Isaiah assumes that a young child can be too ignorant to know good from evil, a fact confirmed by Deuteronomy:

> **"Your children, who you said would be plunder, *your sons who don't yet know good from evil,* will enter there. I will give them the land, and they will take possession of it" (Deuteronomy 1:39, emphasis added).**

According to Moses, there's a time when children are too young to "know good from evil." In other words, it takes a minimal level of knowledge to be capable of responsible moral action.

Paul builds on that point and teases out an important implication:

> **For though her sons had not been born yet *or done anything good or bad,* so that God's purpose according to election might stand (Romans 9:11, emphasis added).**

If you can be too young to *know* good or evil then you can be too young to *do* any good or evil.

In sum, babies are born mortal, but *innocent* (cf. Psalms 106:34-38). And they stay innocent until they eventually reach the point of being able to sin. And the moment they do, they become sinners slouching towards *moral corruption.* Once again, as Moses confirms, people corrupt themselves:

> **"*They have corrupted themselves*; They are not His children, because of their blemish: a perverse and crooked generation" (Deuteronomy 32:5 NKJV, emphasis added).**

God makes men upright—innocent—but then we corrupt ourselves.

G. Sin Results in Mental Corruption

The third effect of sin is *mental corruption.* Sin begins in the mind, and the more you choose to sin, the more corrupt your mind will be. Remember what Paul told the Romans:

> **For though they knew God, they did not glorify him as God or show gratitude. Instead, *their thinking became worthless*, and their senseless hearts were darkened (Romans 1:21, emphasis added).**

People began by knowing the truth about God, but Paul says their thinking *became* worthless, and their hearts *became* darkened, suggesting a decline. Instead of being born that way, they became that way.

Indeed, when people persist in that mental corruption, God gives them over to it:

> **And because they did not think it worthwhile to acknowledge God, God delivered them over to a corrupt mind so that they do what is not right (Romans 1:28).**

Struggling with addictive behavior and thinking patterns is its own punishment.

Related to this, despite sin, the will remains free—at least, free enough to be capable of genuine moral actions for which we are held responsible. Our wills are not immune to corrupting *influences*, but influences are not causes. Sin curbs our choices, but we're still free to make them. Sadly, we often choose to sin.

H. Sin Causes Spiritual Corruption

The fourth effect of sin is *spiritual corruption*, or *spiritual death*. I see that kind of corruption implied by what Paul told the Ephesians:

> **And you were dead in your trespasses and sins (Ephesians 2:1).**

He made a similar comment to the Colossians:

> **And when you were dead in trespasses and in the uncircumcision of your flesh, he made you alive with him and forgave us all our trespasses (Colossians 2:13).**

Paul wasn't talking about physical death, because the Ephesians and Colossians were obviously alive when he wrote to them. Paul was talking about spiritual death. Before they believed, they were physically alive but spiritually dead. Only after they believed in Jesus were they "made alive" in a spiritual sense.

Similarly, when Jesus told Nicodemus that he needed to be born from above by the Spirit (John 3:3), the Lord implied that he was spiritually dead.

Distinguishing between different kinds of death clarifies passages such as Romans 5:12, where Paul is operating with a dual conception of death—one physical and one spiritual.[4] I would bring out Paul's meaning this way:

> **Therefore, just as sin entered the world through one man, and [physical] death through sin, in this way [spiritual] death spread to all people, because all sinned** (Romans 5:12)

In other words, physical death spread to all men through Adam. And that made it possible for everyone to experience spiritual death. What does that kind of spiritual death mean?

Some Free Grace theologians say that it means your human spirit dies. They say that people are created trichotomous (e.g., as spirit, soul, and body, cf. 1 Thessalonians 5:23), but when you sin, you become dichotomous (e.g., reduced to soul and body). Hence, unbelievers need to be regenerated to become trichotomous again (John 3:3, 6).

Given that view, I can imagine an innocent child, created upright by God, but born in a mortal body, growing old enough to be morally accountable, choosing to sin, and experiencing spiritual death for herself. While that view has a certain plausibility to me, I have to admit it's also speculative.

At the very least, being "dead in trespasses and sins" means finding yourself under the shadow of God's future judgment and threatened with what Scripture calls "the second death." Think of it this way. Babies are born innocent. If they die in infancy, I find it hard to believe that God would damn them. Although I'm not absolutely certain that children are automatically saved, that seems like a reasonable answer, all things considered. However, at some point, children are no longer given that allowance. It seems to me that, once a child reaches the age of accountability and chooses to sin, they come under God's condemnation (John 3:18), wrath (John 3:36; Romans 2:5), and judgment (John 5:24, 27). Without Jesus' forgiveness, every unbeliever will die in his sins (John 8:21-26) and be thrown into the lake of fire (Revelation 20:14-15). That is certainly part of what it means to be dead in tresspasses and sins. By contrast, believers are forgiven (Acts 10:43), justified (Galatians 2:16), and have passed from death to life (John 5:24).

We've now covered several different ways in which sin affect us, but careful readers will notice that I have not addressed the issue of *guilt*.

I. You Can't Inherit Guilt

Calvinists and many Arminians claim that we can inherit the original *guilt* of Adam's sin. That theory was built on the ancient pseudo-scientific idea that sin and guilt are passed from father to child through semen. It's bizarre to me that anyone with a modern education would believe that today. It's a classic example of you call a "category mistake." Sin is a moral choice, not a physical substance you can detect under a microscope. Thinking that sin can be passed through semen is like asking how much the color blue weighs. You have your categories mixed up.

In any case, Free Grace rejects the idea of "original guilt" (but remember what I said in the introduction about not speaking for everyone). Indeed, God expressly disavowed the idea that guilt is inheritable:

> **"Fathers are not to be put to death for their children, and children are not to be put to death for their fathers; each person will be put to death for his own sin" (Deuteronomy 14:16).**

Since sin is an individual choice to transgress God's command, the guilt for an action belongs to the person who did it. As Ezekiel confirms:

> **"But you may ask, 'Why doesn't the son suffer punishment for the father's iniquity?' Since the son has done what is just and right, carefully observing all my statutes, he will certainly live. The person who sins is the one who will die. *A son won't suffer punishment for the father's iniquity, and a father won't suffer punishment for the son's iniquity*. The righteousness of the righteous person will be on him, and *the wickedness of the wicked person will be on him*" (Ezekiel 18:19-20, emphasis added).**

According to Ezekiel, who is guilty of sin? *The person who committed it*. If a father breaks the law, the son will not be punished for it (or vice versa). Guilt and righteousness belong to the individuals making moral choices. Doesn't that make sense? If a man in San Francisco robbed a corner store, would it be just to punish a random woman in Toronto for his crime? Of course not. On the contrary, doing that would be the definition of *injustice*.

Inherited guilt is nowhere taught in Scripture.

However, some people think they see it in Psalms 51:5. Admittedly, some translations impose a theology of inherited guilt on the text, such as when the NIV reads, "Surely I was sinful at birth." But that's not what David says or means. Here's the NASB's more literal translation:

> **Behold, I was brought forth in iniquity,**
> **And in sin my mother conceived me (Psalms 51:5 NASB).**

Read that carefully. According to David, who sinned? It was *his mother*. For example, if I said, "In drunkenness, my father beat me," who would you think was drunk—me or my father? My father. Likewise, in a general confession of sin, David said there was even something sinful about his *conception*.

That possibility was discussed in Jewish tradition.

For example, one theory suggested that Jesse might have fathered David either through an adulterous affair or with a prostitute. (Such things had been known to happen, cf. Genesis 38). That might explain why young David wasn't summoned when Samuel called for Jesse's sons, why David's mother is never named, or why David felt "estranged from my brothers" and like "an alien to my mother's sons" (Psalms 69:8).

Other rabbis argued that David's sinful conception had to do with his complicated and questionable Moabite ancestry through Ruth.

In any case, Psalms 51:5 doesn't teach that David was born with a sinful nature, let alone with inherited guilt, let alone that anyone else inherits guilt at birth. You must read that theology into the text.

J. You Can Inherit Consequences

However, while you can't inherit another person's *guilt*, you can inherit the *consequences* of their sin.

We've all suffered from bad decisions made by other people. For example, Adam and Eve passed on death and mortality to all their descendants (cf. Romans 5:12-14). Or think of the children born to the Babylonian exiles who suffered the hardships of being refugees without being personally responsible for Jerusalem's destruction. And then there are children born to alcoholic or drug-addicted mothers who suffer the consequences of those addictions (such as fetal alcohol syndrome), without being personally guilty of drunkenness.

Guilt isn't inheritable, but consequences can be.

K. Able to Seek and to Believe

Sin affects our lives, our world, and everything in it, leading to physical, moral, mental, and spiritual corruption. But does that mean we can't believe in Jesus without being regenerated first? The Biblical answer is clearly "no."

Many passages of Scripture show the unregenerate can seek after God and believe in Him. For example, Luke records a speech that Paul made to the Athenians where he said:

> **"and He made from one man every nation of mankind to live on all the face of the earth, having determined their appointed times and the boundaries of their habitation, *that they would seek God, if perhaps they might grope for Him and find Him,* though He is not far from each one of us" (Acts 17:26-27, emphasis added).**

According to Paul, what can the unregenerate do? They can seek and grope for God and even find Him (i.e., come to faith). One such person was Cornelius the Centurion who is described as—

> **a devout man and one who feared God with all his household, and gave many alms to the Jewish people and prayed to God continually (Acts 10:2).**

Cornelius was searching for God and his prayers were heard (Acts 10:4). We know that Cornelius was unregenerate at this point because as Peter later recalled, he was sent to Cornelius to tell him words "by which you will be saved" (Acts 11:13-14). Cornelius needed salvation. The point is, despite being unsaved, he was still capable of seeking after God.

To give another example, look at how Luke describes Sergius Paulus:

> **He was with the proconsul, Sergius Paulus, an intelligent man. This man summoned Barnabas and Saul and wanted to hear the word of God (Acts 13:7).**

Sergius Paulus wanted to hear the Word of God. He called for Paul (Saul) and Barnabus, heard their message, and believed (Acts 13:12). His seeking preceded his believing.

Clearly, the lost can (and should) seek the Lord, take an interest in the gospel, believe it, and be saved. They don't need to be regenerated fully or partially first.

L. Satan Works to Prevent Faith

The fact that unregenerate people are able to believe and be saved is confirmed by how Satan is actively at work to prevent them from coming to faith:

> **But if our gospel is veiled, it is veiled to those who are perishing. In their case, the god of this age has blinded the minds of the unbelievers to keep them from seeing the light of the gospel of the glory of Christ, who is the image of God (2 Corinthians 4:3-4).**

If Satan is actively blinding the minds of unbelievers to stop them from seeing the light of the gospel, they must be able to believe it. Satan's actions only make sense if total inability is false.

Jesus touched on this topic in His parable of the four soils, saying:

> **"The seed along the path are those who have heard and then the devil comes and takes away the word from their hearts, so that they may not believe and be saved" (Luke 8:12).**

In the parable, the devil rushes in to snatch away the word from their hearts "so that they may not believe and be saved." In other words, both Jesus and the devil assume that unsaved people are capable of hearing and believing the gospel. Coming to faith is not a question of ability, but of willingness.

For example, after Jesus healed a man who had been disabled for thirty-eight years, some of the Jewish leaders objected to healing on the Sabbath, and so decided to persecute Him for it (John 5:16). Suffice to say, they didn't believe in Him! But Jesus didn't blame their inability, but their unwillingness:

> **"But you are not willing to come to me so that you may have life" (John 5:40).**

"Coming" to Jesus here means believing in Him. Jesus is faulting them for failing to do something. These men were able to believe but refused to do it. And they weren't alone. Near the end of His earthly ministry, Jesus wept for the holy city:

> **"Jerusalem, Jerusalem, who kills the prophets and stones those who are sent to her. How often *I wanted* to gather your children together, as a hen gathers her chicks under her wings, *but you were not willing!*" (Matthew 23:37, emphasis added).**

Jesus was willing to save them, but they weren't willing to be saved. If they were unable to believe, then why would the Lord put on a show of weeping over them? If total inability were true, it is hard for me to understand why the Lord would be weeping. I do not believe the Lord was acting. He wept because the tragedy was real. Jerusalem could have been saved but they were unwilling to believe in Jesus, and God held them accountable for that, sending the Romans to destroy the city in AD 66–70.

M. Faith Comes *Before* Regeneration

Instead of teaching that regeneration comes before faith, the Bible consistently teaches that it only comes after someone has believed in Jesus. For example, when Jesus told Nicodemus that he needed to be *born again*, how could he do that? Did it happen before he believed? No. The new birth comes through faith, not before it:

> **"If I have told you about earthly things and you don't *believe*, how will you *believe* if I tell you about heavenly things? No one has ascended into heaven except the one who descended from heaven—the Son of Man.**
>
> **"Just as Moses lifted up the snake in the wilderness, so the Son of Man must be lifted up, so that everyone who *believes* in him may have eternal life. For God loved the world in this way: He gave his one and only Son, so that everyone who *believes* in him will not perish but have eternal life. For God did not send his Son into the world to condemn the world, but to save the world through him. Anyone who *believes* in him is not condemned, but anyone who does *not believe* is already condemned, because he has not *believed* in the name of the one and only Son of God" (John 3:12-18, emphasis added).**

If Nicodemus believed in Jesus, *then* he would have eternal life and be saved (cf. John 3:15-18). Believing comes *before* receiving.

Paul made the same point to the Ephesians. Before believing in Jesus, they were "dead in trespasses and sins," but then God made them "alive" (Ephesians 2:5). How? By grace, through faith:

> **For you are saved by grace through faith, and this is not from yourselves; it is God's gift—not from works, so that no one can boast (Ephesians 2:8-9).**

Salvation comes through faith. This pattern is repeated in every evangelistic presentation in the New Testament. People are saved after they believe in Jesus, not before.

N. God's Initiative in Seeking the Lost

If God doesn't regenerate unbelievers before they come to faith, what is His role in bringing someone to salvation? While I don't see divine determinism in Scripture, I do see that God takes the initiative in salvation, and He does so in several different ways.

First, God *loved* the world before anyone loved Him (John 3:16; 1 John 4:19).

Second, God *planned* for Jesus to be the sacrificial Lamb before the creation of the world (cf. 1 Peter 1:19-20; Revelation 13:8).

Third, Jesus *died* for the whole world (John 1:29; 3:16; 4:42; 2 Peter 2:1; 1 John 2:2).

Fourth, the Lord providentially *arranged* the nations "so that they might seek God" (Acts 17:26-27).

Fifth, instead of being aloof, God is *not far* from every unbeliever. Indeed, they live and move and have their being in Him (Acts 17:27-28).

Sixth, God *sent* His Spirit to convict the world concerning sin, righteousness, and judgment (John 16:8).

Seventh, the only way to come to God is to be *drawn* by the Father (John 6:44). However, Jesus draws *all* men to Himself through the cross (John 12:32), and through listening and learning from the Father (cf. John 6:45). That makes the drawing resistible (cf. Acts 7:51).

Eighth, God *sends* preachers out to the world with the saving message. For example, God sent Peter to Cornelius and Paul to Lydia. But not everyone is willing to believe.

Ninth, based on Lydia's example, God also *opens* the "heart to respond to what Paul was saying" (Acts 16:14). Opening her heart does not mean giving her a new one through regeneration. Instead, one commentator suggested that God "removes any misconception that she has that may prevent her from receiving Christ."[5] In other words, Lydia was already open to the good news, and God removed the remaining obstacles to her response of faith.

In sum, God is actively working to save the world, but not in a deterministic way. Believing in Jesus is preceded by His love, plans, providence, and actions. But nowhere does Scripture teach that unbelievers must be regenerated (in whole or in part) before they come to faith.

O. Conclusion

In the Free Grace view (as I am constructively presenting it), sin leads to physical, mental, moral, and spiritual corruption and, ultimately, to the second death, but it doesn't take away our ability or responsibility to believe in Jesus. Free Grace believes in *liable depravity* but not in *total inability*.

Endnotes

1. Lorraine Boettner, *The Reformed Faith* (Phillipsburg, NJ: Presbyterian and Reformed Publishing Company, 1983), 25.
2. Roger E. Olson, *Arminian Theology: Myths and Realities* (Downers Grove, IL: IVP Academic, 2006), 36.
3. John Walton, *Genesis* (Grand Rapids, MI: Zondervan, 2001, 174.
4. Although I came to this conclusion independently, I'm glad to find it in James D. G. Dunn's *The Theology of Paul* (Grand Rapids, MI: Eerdmans, 1998), 96: "it becomes evident that Paul was operating with a double conception of death. In this case it is the distinction between the death of humanity as an *outcome* of Adam's first transgression and death as a *consequence* or even penalty of one's own individual transgressions. Presumably this ties in with some sort of equivalent distinction between natural death and spiritual death (as in Philo?)."
5. French L. Arrington, "Acts," *Full Life Bible Commentary*, ed. French L. Arrington and Roger Stronstad (Grand Rapids, MI: Zondervan, 1999), 619.

2
Occupational Election

The next point in LOTUS concerns the doctrine of election.

Calvinists and Arminians agree that election is related to eternal salvation.

Calvinists believe that God chooses people more or less arbitrarily to either be saved or damned. As Boettner wrote,

> "God's choice of certain individuals unto salvation before the foundation of the world rested solely in His own sovereign will. His choice of particular sinners was not based on any foreseen response or obedience on their part, such as faith, repentance, etc. On the contrary, God gives faith and repentance to each individual whom He selected."[1]

Meanwhile, Arminians believe God elects people based on their foreseen faith:

> "Only those will be saved, however, who are predestined by God to eternal salvation. They are the elect. Who is included in the elect? All who God foresees will accept his offer of salvation through Christ by not resisting the grace that extends to them through the cross and the gospel."[2]

You see, then, that both traditions agree election is about eternal salvation. But Free Grace has come to—or is increasingly agreeing on—a different conclusion. A careful study of the Biblical evidence reveals the surprising conclusion that God chooses people, places, and things for *service*, not *salvation*. In other words, election is *occupational* (the O in LOTUS).

A. Defining the Key Terms

As far as English is concerned, the word *election* has to do with *choices*. *Electing* someone means to *choose* him. So, for example, whoever who wins a presidential election becomes the *President-elect*.

The Hebrew and Greek words for election are very close to the ordinary English meaning. The primary Hebrew word for election is *bachār* which means "to choose, select, elect, decide for, or prefer."[3] In turn, *bachār* has several derivatives, including *chosen* (*bachir*), *choicest/best* (*mibhār*), and *choice* (*mibhir*). And where Greek is concerned, several words are used to indicate God's *choosing* or *electing*, namely, *eklegomai*, which means *to choose*; *eklektos*, which is the quality *of being elect or chosen*; and *eklektoi*, *the chosen ones*. There are related words, but they all have the general sense of *to choose, appoint*.

Clearly, election is about choosing. The big question is, chosen for what purpose? We'll look at several significant examples of how these keywords are used to help clarify and summarize the evidence.

B. Old Testament Examples

The vocational nature of election is evident throughout the Old Testament, whether studied from the human or divine perspectives.

Human Choices

In the Old Testament, humans elect people, places, and things to serve different purposes. Out of many possible examples, here are three.

First, when Abraham and Lot began to squabble over grazing territory, and decided to go their separate ways, Abraham gave Lot the first choice of where to settle:

> **"So Lot *chose for himself all the valley of the Jordan*, and Lot journeyed eastward. Thus they separated from each other" (Genesis 13:11, emphasis added).**

What did Lot choose? The valley of the Jordan. He obviously didn't choose it for salvation but to serve his purposes.

Second, when Elijah challenged the prophets of Baal to a duel, they chose animals to be sacrificed:

> **"Now let them give us two oxen; and *let them choose one ox***

> ***for themselves* and cut it up, and place it on the wood, but put no fire under it; and I will prepare the other ox and lay it on the wood, and I will not put a fire under it" (1 Kings 18:23, emphasis added).**

The oxen were chosen to be sacrificed, not saved.

Third, when Joshua urged Israel to follow God instead of the neighboring pagan deities he said:

> **"If it is disagreeable in your sight to serve the Lord, *choose for yourselves today whom you will serve*: whether the gods which your fathers served which were beyond the River, or the gods of the Amorites in whose land you are living; but as for me and my house, we will serve the Lord" (Joshua 24:15, emphasis added; cf. Deuteronomy 30:19).**

Although this choice was religious, it was a choice about whom to serve.

That's just a tiny sampling of the evidence, but I hope they make the point that human election is to service, not to eternal salvation.

Now, what about God's election?

God's Choices

Here again, let me give just three representative examples out of many.

First, when Israel was wandering the wilderness, and the people grumbled, there came a point when some usurpers wanted to take over leadership from Moses, and he called on God to decide the matter:

> **"Tomorrow morning the Lord will show who is His, and who is holy, and will bring him near to Himself; *even the one whom He will choose*, He will bring near to Himself'" (Numbers 16:5, emphasis added).**

This was a choice about who would *lead* Israel. In other words, it was vocational. And God made his choice clear when the ground opened up and swallowed the rebels (cf. Numbers 16:31-33).

Second, we're told that God chose Jeremiah to be a prophet:

> **"*I chose you* before I formed you in the womb; I set you apart before you were born. *I appointed you a prophet* to the nations" (Jeremiah 1:5 HCSB, emphasis added).**

Jeremiah wasn't chosen for eternal life but to serve as "a prophet to the nations."

Third, God not only elected *individuals* to serve Him, but He could also choose *places*, the most obvious being Jerusalem:

> **"When Your people go out to battle against their enemy, wherever You send them, and when they pray to the Lord *toward the city which You have chosen* and the temple which I have built for Your name" (1 Kings 8:44, emphasis added).**

Furthermore, as a sign of Jerusalem's election, God had the Temple built there, which was also elected by God (see 2 Chronicles 7:16). I'm sure you realize that cities and temples are not chosen for salvation but to serve God's purposes.

Choosing Groups Through Individuals
As you study election in the Old Testament, you'll begin to notice a pattern. Oftentimes, when God chose an *individual* to serve Him, He'd implicitly choose *a corporate body* to continue that service. For example, when God chose Abraham, He also elected the Jewish people to be the chosen nation. When He chose Aaron to serve as high priest, He implicitly chose his family and tribe to serve as Aaronite and Levitical priests. And finally, when God elected David as king, He also implicitly chose David's family to be the royal house (2 Samuel 6:21; 1 Kings 8:16; 1 Chronicles 28:4).

In other words, later Jews, priests, and kings participated in the election of their ancestors. And let me emphasize that these were not elections *to salvation* since not every Jew, priest, or member of David's house was saved. Only believers are saved. Instead, these were corporate elections *to service*. We'll see this individual/corporate pattern later when we discuss Jesus and the Church.

C. New Testament Examples

The New Testament evidence about election complements the Old Testament evidence. Once again, let's examine both human and divine examples of election.

Human Choices
Where human election is concerned, here are two representative examples.

First, when Jesus visited Bethany, Martha became irritated at how her sister Mary preferred to listen to Jesus rather than help with the guests. But Jesus said, "Mary has chosen the good part" (Luke 10:41-42). This was a choice to sit under the Lord's teaching.

Second, when Paul and Barnabus disagreed over whether to bring Mark along for the journey, the two men parted ways, and "Paul chose Silas" (Acts 15:40) to be his new partner in ministry. Once again, this was a choice to service.

Is divine election any different? You might assume that now we'll finally get to the evidence that clearly shows God chooses individuals for salvation or damnation. If so, you'd be wrong.

Divine Choices

Here are four examples of divine election to service in the New Testament.

First, Jesus chose twelve men to be apostles (Luke 6:13). We read that "He *appointed* twelve," not for salvation, but to "send them out *to preach*" (emphasis added). We know this was not an election to eternal life because Judas was chosen to be an apostle, and he was "a devil" (John 6:70; cf. John 13:10).

Second, the vocational nature of election is also illustrated by how Christ "*appointed* seventy others" to preach in "every city and place where He Himself was going to come" (Luke 10:1, emphasis added). Once again, they were chosen to serve.

Third, after Jesus rose from the dead, He appeared "to witnesses chosen before by God" (Acts 10:41). What were they chosen for? They were selected to serve as witnesses to the resurrection, not to have eternal life.

Fourth, and lastly, consider Paul, whom Jesus selected to be "*a chosen instrument* of Mine, to bear My name before the Gentiles and kings and the sons of Israel'" (Acts 9:15, emphasis added). The Greek word for "instrument" refers to a serving dish, which is as clear an image of occupational election as you can get.

I think you'll find that wherever people are chosen in the New Testament, it's almost always to some kind of service.

D. Jesus Is the Chosen One

The fact that election is to service, not to salvation, is most obvious in the case of Jesus. In Matthew's Gospel, Jesus is identified as the long-awaited Messiah whose coming was foretold by Isaiah. And what is His title?

> **"Behold, My Servant, whom I uphold; *My chosen one* in whom My soul delights" (Matthew 12:18; cf. Isaiah 42:1, emphasis added).**

Jesus is the prime example of being "chosen" by God. Even the taunts of His persecutors show He was commonly known as the Chosen One:

> **"He saved others; let Him save Himself if this is the Christ of God, *His Chosen One*" (Luke 23:35b, emphasis added).**

But what was Jesus chosen for? Not to be saved! After all, He *is* the Savior. And it wasn't to have eternal life because He *is* eternal life (cf. John 14:6; 1 John 5:11). Jesus was chosen to serve as the Messiah. God's choice had redemptive purposes, in view, but his election was for service, not salvation.

E. The Nations in Romans 9

A popular passage of Scripture that is commonly (mis)used to teach that God chooses individuals to eternal life or death is Romans 9. That approach completely misses Paul's argument.

In Romans 9–11, Paul answers numerous objections he heard during his missionary work in the synagogues. How could Jesus be the Messiah if Israel has mostly rejected Him? Has God abandoned Israel? Is He unfaithful to the promises He made?

Paul more or less throws the kitchen sink at those objections.

His answer in Romans 9 is to show that it has always been God's prerogative to use different groups of people to serve His purposes—even Gentiles.

People often miss the corporate nature of Paul's argument because they fail to look up his Old Testament allusions.

For example, Paul talks about how Esau was chosen to serve Jacob, but his quote from Malachi 1:2-3 makes clear he's thinking about Israel and Edom.

The reference to Pharaoh is about how God used Egypt as a nation to punish and bless Israel.

And Paul's reference to the potter and the clay is taken from prophesies in Isaiah and Jeremiah relating to how God used Babylon to punish Israel.

Paul's point is that the Jews shouldn't be surprised if God is choosing the Gentiles right now since He has always exercised the prerogative to choose groups of people to serve His purposes.

In sum, Romans 9 has nothing to do with choosing individuals for eternal life or death and everything with God's choice of nations to serve His purposes.

F. Chosen in Christ

There's one passage that comes close to teaching an election to salvation, but not in the way you would expect. In Ephesians, Paul's argument is that God chooses people *in Christ*:

> **For he chose us in him, before the foundation of the world, to be holy and blameless in love before him (Eph 1:4).**

Paul does not say God chose us *to be in Him*. He says He chose us *in Him*. Paul uses that language multiple times throughout Ephesians 1 and 2 where you see phrases like "in Christ" (1:3), "in Him" (1:4), "by Jesus Christ" (1:5), "in the Beloved" (1:6), "in Him" (1:7), "in Himself" (1:9), "in Christ/in Him" (1:10), "in Him" (1:11a), "in Him (1:11b), "in Christ" (1:12), and so on. This is the language of union with Christ.

Do you recognize the individual/corporate pattern of election here? Just as the Jews were chosen through Abraham, the Aaronites were chosen through Aaron, and the kings were chosen through David, we are chosen through Christ. As William Klein says, "Christ is the principally elected one and God has chosen a corporate body to be included in him."[4]

I appreciate how Beals and Radmacher explain how that works:

> "When I believed, at that point I was placed *in Christ*. I become in God's sight what Jesus is. At the time of the conscious act of faith, through becoming one with Christ, I was chosen *in Him*. I was not chosen to believe, but having believed I was chosen *for all that He is*. Is Christ without sin in the reckoning of the Father? So am I (Eph 1:4, 7). Is Christ risen from the dead? In the reckoning of God, even now so am I (Eph 2:6), although the event waits the Lord's reappearing (1 Cor 15:51-52). Was Christ chosen before the foundation of the world? So am I, although my being chosen did not take place until the day that through faith I was placed 'in him.' As a believer I was chosen 'before the foundation of the world,' but only through being 'in Him.'"[5]

Everyone who believes in Jesus participates in His election and enjoys everything that comes from union with Christ. But that is very different from an individual election to salvation or damnation.

G. Election and Free Will

One of the thorniest questions about election debates concerns reconciling God's sovereignty with man's free will. Calvinists and Arminians have different answers to the problem. But when you see that election is to service, it changes the nature of the question.

Where God's *sovereignty* is concerned, He freely chooses who will serve and how they will serve. No one can prevent or compel God's choices. If God chooses Jeremiah or John the Baptist to be prophets, they can't refuse God's election.

However, servants are free to be faithful or unfaithful in their service. While Joshua, Josiah, and Paul chose to be faithful in their service, Moses, King Saul, and Judas freely chose to rebel.

Put simply, God is sovereign in His choosing, and the servant is responsible for his performing.

H. Conclusion

Sometimes, the Bible and theologians can talk past each other, and I think that's what happened with election. Despite what Calvinists and Arminians insist, Biblical election is of people, places, and things to *service*, not to *salvation*.[6] Election is occupational.

Endnotes

1. Boettner, *The Reformed Faith* (Phillipsburg, NJ: Presbyterian and Reformed Publishing Company, 1983), 26.
2. Roger E. Olson, *Arminian Theology: Myths and Realities* (Downers Grove, IL: IVP Academic, 2006), 35.
3. R. Laird Harris, Gleason L. Archer, Jr., Bruce K. Waltke, *Theological Workbook of the Old Testament* (Chicago, IL: Moody, 1980), 100; *Mounce's Complete Expository Dictionary of Old & New Testament Words*, eds. William D. Mounce, D. Matthew Smith, Miles Van Pelt (Grand Rapids, MI: Zondervan, 2006), 107.
4. William Klein, *The New Chosen People: A Corporate View of Election* (Grand Rapids, MI: Zondervan, 1990), 180.
5. R. S. Beals, Jr. and Earl D. Radmacher, *Ephesians: Life and Love in Christ* (Chino Valley, AZ: One World Press, 2012), 14-15.
6. For a much fuller treatment, see my book *Chosen to Serve: Why Divine Election Is to Service, Not to Eternal Life* (Denton, TX: Grace Evangelical Society, 2017).

3
Tiered Atonement

The next petal in the flower concerns the cross and what it accomplished. Paul told the Corinthians that he resolved "to know nothing among you except Jesus Christ and him crucified" (1 Corinthians 2:2). The cross was at the center of Paul's preaching. But what, exactly, did it accomplish?

Most Calvinists say Christ's death was sufficient for all but only ever meant for the elect. They believe in *limited atonement*, meaning Jesus only died for the elect. According to Boettner: "Christ's redeeming work was intended to save the elect only and actually secured salvation for them."[1]

By contrast, Arminians and 4-Point Calvinists say the cross was sufficient for all, and its benefits are offered to all, but only those who meet the condition(s) of salvation get the benefits. They believe in *unlimited atonement*. As Olson explains,

> "the atoning death of Christ is universal; some of its benefits are automatically extended to all (e.g., release from the condemnation of Adam's sin) and all of its benefits are for everyone who accepts them (e.g., forgiveness of actual sins and imputation of righteousness)."[2]

In many ways I lean towards the unlimited atonement view, as do most Free Grace people. However, as I struggled through this issue, I realized that both positions were making a big assumption. Generally speaking (there are always exceptions), both assumed the benefits of the cross *come as a package* which they then debated was either limited or unlimited. Is that a safe assumption? Is it Biblical?

After careful study, I've concluded that the cross's benefits don't come as a package at all. Instead, you could say there are different tiers of benefits meant for different people given under different conditions. Hence, I call this the *tiered atonement theory*. Let me show you why that's a more fruitful approach to the cross and its benefits.

A. The Levitical Sacrifices

Let's start with the Levitical sacrifices. The Law commanded the people to make several different sacrifices and offerings in the tabernacle and temple. What were they, what benefits did they give, and did those benefits come as one big package?

First, *the burnt offerings* of a bull, ram, or dove were made for unintentional sins or as an expression of worship (Leviticus 1).

Second, *the grain offerings* recognized God's goodness and provisions (Leviticus 2).

Third, *the peace offering* was for thanksgiving and fellowship (Leviticus 3).

Fourth, *the sin offering* was a mandatory sacrifice for specific unintentional sins and for cleansing from defilement (Leviticus 4).

Sixth, *the trespass offering* was for unintentional sins that required restitution (Leviticus 5:14–6:7).

Seventh, on *the Day of Atonement*, the high priest would make a personal sin offering of a bull for himself and his family. Then he would enter the Holy of Holies and sacrifice a goat for the nation of Israel, letting a second scapegoat go free (Leviticus 16).

Put simply, there were different sacrifices, with different benefits, for different people, given under different conditions. Some sacrifices had individual benefits; others, corporate. Some were for families; others, for the nation. Some were for citizens; others for priests. Some were for forgiveness; others, for thanksgiving.

Although that doesn't prove the cross follows the same pattern, it does confirm that the tiered approach has a Biblical precedent. As we look at a sampling of the New Testament evidence, let's ask three questions. First, what is the benefit? Second, who is the beneficiary? And third, what is the condition for receiving the benefit?

B. Genesis 3:15

Soon after the creation of the world, a serpent appeared in the Garden and seduced Adam and Eve to sin. After their fall, God gave the first promise of a coming Redeemer:

> **"I will put hostility between you and the woman,**
> **and between your offspring and her offspring.**
> **He will strike your head,**
> **and you will strike his heel" (Genesis 3:15).**

Benefit: Killing the serpent.
Beneficiary: God(?).
Condition: The offspring being struck on the heel.
Interpretation: Christian theologians have taken Genesis 3:15 to be the first promise of the gospel in Scripture. In Eden, the serpent (whom we know to be Satan, cf. Revelation 12:9), struck a blow against God's creation by prompting the fall of man. In response, God promised to strike Satan back. There would be "hostility" between the serpent and the woman—a war between two seed lines. The woman would have an offspring (i.e., the Messiah), and while the serpent would strike Him on the heel (alluding to the cross), He would deliver a killing blow to the serpent's head.

One of the benefits of the cross is victory over Satan. In other words, the promise situates the cross in a larger narrative of a battle between God and Satan for the dominion of creation. You could say it's a battle between the Dragon and the Lamb. The cross was a pivotal moment in that war, bringing victory to God.

C. Colossians 2:14-15

The theme of God's battle with Satan, which some have called "the angelic conflict," is taken up in Paul's letter to the Colossians, where he explained that through the cross, Christ defeated His spiritual enemies:

> **He erased the certificate of debt, with its obligations, that was against us and opposed to us, and has taken it away by nailing it to the cross. He disarmed the rulers and authorities and disgraced them publicly; he triumphed over them in him (Colossians 2:14-15).**

Benefit: (1) Erasing the certificate of debt; (2) Disarming, disgracing, and triumphing over rulers and authorities.
Beneficiary: (1) Believers; (2) God.
Condition: The cross.
Interpretation: In our rationalistic age, we may be tempted to doubt

or downplay the spiritual warfare aspect of salvation. The exorcisms performed by Jesus, the apostles, and others show that the spiritual battle is real and that it's central to the meaning of the cross.

Focusing on the second benefit, Paul used military imagery to depict God's victory. He "disarmed" the powers, which paints the picture of stripping an enemy soldier of his armor. Then God "disgraced them publicly," which evokes the image of a general leading a victory parade of defeated captives, exposing them to the public scorn of the onlooking crowds. That's what happened to the fallen spiritual powers at Christ's crucifixion.

D. Revelation 5:9-10

Christ's victory on the cross qualified Him to do something else. Listen to this song from the book of Revelation:

> **And they sang a new song:**
> **"You are worthy to take the scroll**
> **and to open its seals,**
> **because you were slaughtered,**
> **and you purchased people**
> **for God by your blood**
> **from every tribe and language**
> **and people and nation.**
> **You made them a kingdom**
> **and priests to our God,**
> **and they will reign on the earth" (Revelation 5:9-10).**

Benefit: (1) Being worthy to open the scroll; (2) purchasing a people for God.

Beneficiary: Jesus.

Condition: The death of Christ.

Interpretation: First, Jesus received the benefit of being worthy of opening the scroll. What is the scroll, and what does it mean for Him to open it? Commentators have offered a variety of answers, suggesting it may be a scroll containing all the works of men, or the Lamb's book of life, or God's general plans for human destiny. When the contents are revealed in Revelation 6, it deals primarily with events of judgments. As Beale says, "The book is thus best understood as containing God's plan of judgment and redemption, which has been set in motion by Christ's death and resurrection but has yet to be completed."[3] Whatever the case, one benefit of the cross is that Jesus became qualified to open the scroll.

But second, Christ's death purchased a people through his blood. If the cross qualified Him to open the scroll of judgment on unbelievers, it also enabled Him to save a people for Himself. God created mankind to rule over creation (cf. Genesis 1:26-28). When we fell, Satan became the god of this age (cf. 2 Corinthians 4:4), and sinners became citizens of a kingdom of darkness (cf. Colossians 1:13). Through the cross, Jesus bought a people to be a new kingdom of priests who will reign with Him on earth, effectively reversing what was lost at the fall.

E. Romans 3:25

Yet another benefit is presented in Paul's letter to the Romans. The apostle had not founded the Roman church, so he sent a letter summarizing his gospel preaching in the hopes they would help with his planned mission to Spain (Rom 15:24). When Paul explained the meaning of Christ's death, he said it had a public purpose:

> **God presented him as the mercy seat by his blood, through faith, to demonstrate his righteousness, because in his restraint God passed over the sins previously committed (Romans 3:25).**

Benefit: To publicly demonstrate God's righteousness.
Beneficiary: (1) God; (2) The world.
Condition: The cross.

Interpretation: Given the many sins of humanity (described by Paul in grisly detail in Rom 1:18—3:20), why did it seem like God let people get away with it? Was God unjust? According to Paul, the cross is God's answer to those complaints. Through it God demonstrated His righteousness to the world. God *presented* Jesus as a sacrifice in a public way. Some translations say He is the *propitiation* for sin, meaning He turns away God's wrath. Others, like the CSB above, suggest Jesus was presented as *the mercy seat*, a reference to part of the Ark of the Covenant, where sins were atoned for, and God's wrath was averted. For Paul, the cross replaces the Ark. Instead of having a yearly ritual hidden from view in the Temple, God made atonement publicly on the cross, showing everyone that He didn't pass over sin, but punished it through Jesus. The world benefits by seeing God's righteousness, and God benefits by demonstrating it.

F. Romans 3:26

In the next verse, Paul mentioned a second benefit:

> **God presented him to demonstrate his righteousness at the present time, so that he would be just and justify the one who has faith in Jesus (Rom 3:26).**

Benefit: (1) Being just; (2) Getting justification.
Beneficiary: (1) God; (2) The one who has faith.
Condition: Faith in Jesus.

Interpretation: Since God has publicly demonstrated His righteousness through the cross, He's now free to justify anyone on the basis of faith, apart from works, without seeming to be unjust or soft on sin. And if you avail yourself of Jesus as the new mercy seat by believing in Him, you get the benefit of being reckoned righteous before God (cf. Galatians 2:16).

G. John 3:14-15

God not only justifies believers, but He also gives them new life. In His famous dialogue with Nicodemus, Jesus said the rabbi needed many different things. Jesus spoke of entering the kingdom, seeing the kingdom, being born from above, not being condemned, not perishing, and, of course, having eternal life. In that conversation, Jesus also alluded to the cross. Nicodemus would not have understood the full meaning of Jesus' words, but John's readers would have understood the comparison between Moses lifting up the bronze serpent and Jesus being lifted up on the cross. The point was, just as the Israelites were saved by a single glance at the serpent on the pole, people would be saved through faith in Him:

> **"So, just as Moses lifted up the snake in the desert, in the same way the son of man must be lifted up, so that everyone who believes in him may share in the life of God's new age" (John 3:14-15 NTFE).**

Benefit: Life of God's new age.
Beneficiary: Whoever.
Condition: Believe in Him.

Interpretation: While many translations say "eternal life" here, I'm growing to appreciate the more literal translation, "the life of God's new age." It emphasizes the eschatological nature of salvation.

A kingdom is coming! Although we live in a present evil age (cf. Galatians 1:4), we're hoping for an age to come (Luke 20:35; cf. Matthew 12:32) when Christ will resurrect us to new life (John 11:24-27), and He will reign forever. The cross makes that life possible, and everyone who believes in Jesus will have it.

H. Hebrews 2:18

Some benefits are given to believers at the point of salvation, while others are for living the Christian life. For example:

> **For it is clear that he does not reach out to help angels, but to help Abraham's offspring. Therefore, he had to be like his brothers and sisters in every way, so that he could become a merciful and faithful high priest in matters pertaining to God, to make atonement for the sins of the people. For since he himself has suffered when he was tempted, he is able to help those who are tempted (Hebrews 2:16-18, emphasis added).**

Benefit: Help during temptation.
Beneficiary: Those who are tempted (i.e., believers).
Condition: Not explained.
Interpretation: The Son of God became a man for specific reasons. First, to be a merciful and faithful high priest. Second, to make atonement for sins. And third, to give help to those who are tempted. That last point is an ongoing benefit that believers can potentially enjoy. The Lord experienced all the temptations that we experience and more, such as those unique to His vocation as the Messiah. Thanks to that, Jesus can help us to overcome our temptations. How He does that isn't clear, and we know from experience that it isn't irresistible. However, to name another ongoing benefit, if we succumb to temptation and choose to sin, Jesus also acts as our Advocate with the Father (cf. 1 John 2:1).

I. Summary

There are dozens of the cross's benefits that we could have looked at, but I hope you can see from this selection that they don't come as one big package that is either limited or unlimited. Instead, they seem to come in tiers of related benefits: to God in his war with Satan, to Christ in vocation as Messiah, to the unbelieving world in its questions about God's righteousness, to the believer at the point of salvation, and finally, to the disciple in living the Christian life.

J. Theories of the Atonement

A tiered approach to the cross's benefits also touches on the debates about the different theories of atonement. You can study the cross in terms of its individual benefits or consider a bird's-eye view of how the cross works. To that end, theologians propose different theories to explain it, the most popular of which are the penal substitution view, ransom theory, *Christus Victor*, satisfaction theory, the governmental view, and the moral influence view.

Theologians will often say that only one theory can be true. I think you can already guess my objection: that assumes the benefits of the cross come as a package that can be exhaustively explained by only one theory. When you see there are different tiers of benefits, you can imagine how different types of benefits might be explained by different theories.

For example, Christ being crushed for our sins is certainly an example of penal substitution (Isaiah 53:5). Christ ransoming us fits the ransom view (1 Peter 1:18). Christ disarming the evil cosmic powers is an example of the *Christus Victor* model (Colossians 2:15). And God's presenting Jesus as a demonstration of His righteousness agrees with the governmental view (Romans 3:25-26).

Since no single view is exhaustive of all the benefits of the cross, I think Free Grace people should take advantage of each theory of the atonement to help explain what our Savior has done.

K. Double-Jeopardy

I opened this section by highlighting a major assumption being made by Calvinists and Arminians about the cross. They also make a second big assumption, namely, adopting the legal principle of *double jeopardy*. English Common Law developed the idea that once a defendant is acquitted, convicted, or punished for a crime, he can't be prosecuted for it again. Americans learn that moral principle through the Fifth Amendment of the United States Constitution. Calvinists and Arminians have taken that modern legal principle and applied it to the logic of the cross.

So, for example, Calvinists reason that Jesus couldn't have actually paid for the sins of the world because then people in hell would be paying a second time for sin, violating double jeopardy. They conclude that Christ must have only died for the sins of the elect.

Meanwhile, (some) Arminians solve the problem by claiming that Jesus only potentially paid for the sins of the world. The payment is available but only applied to those who fulfill the condition(s) of salvation. Otherwise, they pay for their own sins in hell.

Who is right?

Once again, I doubt both options because I doubt that double jeopardy is a Biblical principle. The fact that it took centuries for the Common Law to develop that legal principle means earlier people had different moral and legal convictions. Although I see double jeopardy in the U.S. Constitution, I haven't been able to find it in the Bible. In fact, I think I see a different intuition at play. For example, look what happens at the end of Jesus' parable of the unforgiving servant:

> **"Then, after he had summoned him, his master said to him, 'You wicked servant! I forgave you all that debt because you begged me. Shouldn't you also have had mercy on your fellow servant, as I had mercy on you?' And because he was angry, his master handed him over to the jailers to be tortured until he could pay everything that was owed. So also my heavenly Father will do to you unless every one of you forgives his brother or sister from your heart" (Matthew 18:32-35).**

In v 32, the master says he "forgave" the servant's debt. In other words, he was acquitted. But then, in v 34, the master reverses that forgiveness, re-instates the debt, and hands the servant over to the jailers to be tortured until he paid back everything that he owed. Jesus warned the Father would do the same thing to unforgiving people. If the Bible assumed double jeopardy, God couldn't act that way. But since He does, double jeopardy must not be a Biblical principle upon which to base our atonement theology.

L. Conclusion

Even though I've only surveyed a handful of the cross's benefits, I hope that I've established they don't come as a package that is either limited or unlimited. That's a false dichotomy. A better approach is to see that the cross has different tiers of benefits aimed at different beneficiaries and enjoyed under different conditions.

Endnotes

1. Lorraine Boettner, *The Reformed Faith* (Phillipsburg, NJ: Presbyterian and Reformed Publishing Company, 1983), 26.
2. Roger E. Olson, *Arminian Theology: Myths and Realities*

(Downers Grove, IL: IVP Academic, 2006), 34.
3. G. K. Beale with David H. Campbell, *Revelation: A Shorter Commentary* (Grand Rapids, MI: Eerdmans, 2015), 111.

4

Undeserved Grace

Everyone claims to believe in salvation by grace, but look carefully and those claims usually die the death of a thousand qualifications. Two errors are widespread. On the one hand, preachers *front-load the gospel* by explicitly teaching that you're saved by faith plus works. On the other hand, preachers *back-load the gospel* when they redefine faith to include doing good works. Either view makes works a condition of salvation, and therefore preaches "a different gospel" (Galatians 1:6).

I know there are teachers outside of the Free Grace camp who clearly teach salvation by faith apart from works and mean it. It is not exclusive to us. However, while there is ambiguity in other traditions, the Free Grace position clearly and consistently teaches salvation by *underserved grace.*

A. What Calvinists and Arminians Mean By "Grace"

Calvinists talk about irresistible grace. While they use the word *grace* and even speak about "the doctrines of grace" they're really talking about *divine determinism*. In their view, for salvation to be by "grace" means that God must predestine or cause it to happen without any free cooperation from creatures—not even at the level of faith. In fact, Calvinists will say if salvation depended on someone freely believing, that would turn faith itself into a work. So, they reason, faith must be caused by God if salvation is to be by grace. For example, J. I. Packer explained that if we were free to believe, then we would be relying upon ourselves for salvation:

> "for to rely on oneself for faith is no different in principle from relying on oneself for works, and the one is as un-Christian and anti-Christian as the other."[1]

Hence, according to Calvinism, if people could freely believe, that kind of faith would count as salvation by works. In order for grace to be grace, salvation must be entirely monergistic, from the Greek meaning "one" (*mon*) "work" (*erg*).[2] It must be caused by God.

Meanwhile, Arminians also claim to believe in grace but often think of it as a power to cooperate with until the end of your life. The fourth article of the Remonstance (an Arminian confession) called it "this co-operating grace."[3] You receive "grace" through various means (e.g., preaching, the sacraments), and if you take advantage of those means, persevering in faith and good works until death, you can be saved. R. Larry Shelton, a Wesleyan theologian explained:

> "Every aspect of salvation, from the first awareness of moral need to ultimate consummation in glorification is worked through God's grace. ...[t]here is a cooperation, or synergism, between divine grace and the human will. The Spirit of God does not work irresistibly, but through the concurrence of the free will of individuals. Finally, salvation is all of grace. Although the human will must respond to the offer of grace at every level of spiritual development, the will does not initiate or merit grace or salvation."[4]

Notice that Shelton says that salvation is *synergistic*, from the Greek "work" (*erg*) "together" (*syn*). According to most Arminians, if you fail to continuously cooperate with God's grace, you can either lose your salvation or fail to be saved.

By contrast, the Free Grace position believes that salvation is given by grace, through faith, apart from any kind of "ergism."

Since everyone says they believe in grace, it is easy to hear someone say the word and assume you both mean the same thing by it. Since that is seldom the case, let's build an inductive case for the Free Grace approach to salvation by grace.

B. A Biblical Definition of Grace

Despite what is often assumed, grace is not a synonym for determinism or monergism. Instead, it translates the Greek word *charis*, which means "a favorable attitude toward someone or something,"[5] or "a beneficent disposition toward someone, favor, grace, gracious care/

help, goodwill."[6] Grace is *God's mental attitude of favor*. Sometimes, God's favor is merited, and at other times, it's not. But as far as salvation is concerned, God's favor is unmerited. We know that because Paul said it was given apart from our works:

> **For you are saved by grace through faith, and this is not from yourselves; it is God's gift—not from works, so that no one can boast (Ephesians 2:8-9).**

Not from works. Period. You can't earn salvation. You can only receive it as a gift through faith. Indeed, Paul made it clear that this kind of grace excludes works:

> **Now if by grace, then it is not by works; otherwise grace ceases to be grace (Romans 11:6).**

Grace and works are mutually exclusive. Salvation is by one or the other, but never both.

Oftentimes, Free Grace is mockingly dismissed as "cheap grace." But do you see why that's wrong? If salvation was cheap, it would still cost something. But the truth is, it doesn't cost us anything at all—it's a gift! Jesus paid the full price for our salvation so that the one and only condition to be saved is to believe in Him—no works required.

And do you see what that charge reveals about the critics? If they reject "cheap" grace, they must believe in "costly" grace, which means they think that salvation is either earned, kept, or maintained by works. And that shows the critics don't believe in grace at all because, as Paul exhausted language to explain, *grace excludes works*.

To be absolutely clear: salvation isn't *cheap*, it's *free*. Hence, the name of our position—Free Grace.

C. What It Means to Believe

The one and only condition of eternal salvation is *to believe in Jesus* (earthly salvation is a different issue). Salvation by faith alone isn't an obscure doctrine built upon one or two verses but is clearly stated in dozens of verses.[7]

Unfortunately, I've found that many people claim to believe in salvation by faith alone redefine faith to include doing works. A fashionable definition today is that faith means "allegiance to Christ," which requires works. Or they'll say we can only be saved by a living faith, and a living faith works. That couldn't be more wrong or destructive to the gospel.

The verb for *believe* (*pisteuō*) means "think to be true, to believe, implying trust."[8] Another lexicon says it means "to consider something to be true and therefore worthy of one's trust, believe."[9] If you consider a claim or promise to be true, then you believe it. If you think it's false, then you don't.

Abraham is a good example of what it means to believe. Here's how he responded to God's promise:

> ***He did not weaken in faith* when he considered his own body to be already dead (since he was about a hundred years old) and also the deadness of Sarah's womb. *He did not waver in unbelief* at God's promise but was strengthened in his faith and gave glory to God, because *he was fully convinced that what God had promised, he was also able to do*. Therefore, it was credited to him for righteousness (Rom 4:19-21, emphasis added).**

God promised Abraham a son, and despite being far too old to have children, he was *fully convinced* that God would keep His promise. That's what it means to believe: *to be convinced or persuaded that something is true.*

Much confusion is created by teachers who claim to believe in salvation by faith and who then muddy (or poison!) the waters by falsely claiming there are different ways to believe (e.g., heart vs head; demon faith vs obedience faith; gift faith vs natural faith, etc). That's all dangerous nonsense that robs believers of their assurance. There is only one way to believe: to be persuaded.

However, while there's only one way to believe, there are millions of different things you can believe. For example, you can believe that Cajun food is better than Mexican food, that playing baseball is more fun than going to the dentist, or that the Federal Reserve is devaluing the dollar. Those are all examples of *faith*, but not *saving faith*. To be saved, you must be convinced of something specific. It's not enough to believe in, say, monotheism, which even the demons are persuaded is true (cf. James 2:19). To be saved, you must believe the gospel is true. Peter was sent to Cornelius with "a message…by which you and all your household will be saved" (Acts 11:14). Of course, that is a message about Jesus, to bring people to faith in Jesus. If you're persuaded that the gospel message is true, then you'll be saved.

Look at how Luke draws a contrast between different responses to the gospel:

> **Some were *persuaded* by what he said, but others *did not believe* (Acts 28:24, emphasis added).**

The Greek for *persuaded* is *peithō* which means "to believe in something or someone to the extent of placing reliance or trust in or on."[10] That's the same definition as believing, which is why Luke uses it as a synonym. When Paul evangelized, Luke says he sought to persuade Jews and Gentiles of the truth:

> **He reasoned in the synagogue every Sabbath and tried *to persuade* both Jews and Greeks (Acts 18:4, emphasis added).**

> **Paul entered the synagogue and spoke boldly over a period of three months, arguing and *persuading them* about the kingdom of God (Acts 19:8, emphasis added).**

Why was Paul trying to persuade them? Because faith and persuasion are synonyms. To believe is to be persuaded. Understanding that prevents so much gospel confusion.

D. Salvation Is Not by Works

When faith is redefined to include doing good works, you lose the gospel. Since believing and behaving are two different actions, Paul could proclaim that we're saved by one and not the other. If believing included working, Paul could not make the arguments he did.

The apostle exhausted the possibilities of language trying to teach the Galatians that simple truth:

> **and yet because we know that a person is not justified by the works of the law but by faith in Jesus Christ, even we ourselves have believed in Christ Jesus. This was so that we might be justified by faith in Christ and not by the works of the law, because by the works of the law no human being will be justified (Galatians 2:16).**

Read that carefully. Can you sense his frustration? People find this simple point so difficult to understand. Three times Paul says we know that we're not justified by works, and three times he says that we're justified by faith. Why is that so hard to understand?

Elsewhere, Paul made the same point that no one would ever be justified before God on the basis of their obedience to the law:

> **Now it is clear that no one is justified before God by the law, because the righteous will live by faith (Galatians 3:11).**

To clarify, we're not only just justified apart from our *bad* works, but apart from our very *best* works:

> **he saved us—not by works of righteousness that we had done, but according to his mercy—through the washing of regeneration and renewal by the Holy Spirit (Titus 3:5).**

No amount of "works of righteousness" can save you. Even your best works are as filthy as menstrual rags (Isa 64:6). No wonder, then, that salvation must be by His mercy and not at all based on what we deserve. As Paul told the Romans, the power of the gospel is that it is by *faith*, *faith*, and *faith*:

> **For in it the righteousness of God is revealed from *faith* to *faith*, just as it is written: The righteous will live by *faith* (Romans 1:17, emphasis added).**

Can Scripture be any clearer? Believe and be saved.

E. Too Sinful to Be Saved by Works

The fact that salvation is by faith apart from works is supported by Scripture's evaluation of our personal righteousness. When you realize that God's standard is perfection, you'll see why no one could ever merit it based on works. Do you think you're a basically good person? Listen again to Jesus' judgment of humanity:

> **"Why do you call me good?" Jesus asked him. "No one is good except God alone" (Mark 10:18).**

No one is good. No one. Jesus is talking about goodness in the *absolute* sense, not a *relative* sense. Yes, as measured against society's expectations, there are relatively good fathers and mothers and nurses and firefighters and so on. But measured against God's perfection, no one is good except Him alone, including believers. (Jesus is the exception because He is God, John 1:1; 20:28). As Paul strongly concurred:

> **There is no one righteous, not even one.**
> **There is no one who understands;**
> **there is no one who seeks God.**
> **All have turned away;**

> **all alike have become worthless.**
> **There is no one who does what is good,**
> **not even one (Romans 3:10-12).**

How can bad people expect to be saved based on being good? It's a spiritual delusion—a sign that they don't understand their true condition as sinners in need of a total Savior. It also shows they're still trusting in their own righteousness instead of in Christ alone.

Jesus told a parable about such people:

> **He also told this parable *to some who trusted in themselves that they were righteous* and looked down on everyone else: "Two men went up to the temple to pray, one a Pharisee and the other a tax collector. The Pharisee was standing and praying like this about himself: 'God, I thank you that I'm not like other people—greedy, unrighteous, adulterers, or even like this tax collector. I fast twice a week; I give a tenth of everything I get.'**
>
> **"But the tax collector, standing far off, would not even raise his eyes to heaven but kept striking his chest and saying, 'God, have mercy on me, a sinner!' I tell you, *this one went down to his house justified rather than the other*, because everyone who exalts himself will be humbled, but the one who humbles himself will be exalted" (Luke 18:9-14, emphasis added).**

According to Jesus, who was justified before God? Not the Pharisee who trusted in his own good works, but the tax collector who didn't.

And notice that Jesus drew a contrast between trusting in your works and trusting in God—*you cannot do both at once*. You might think you can, but God says no, so stop it:

> **But to the one *who does not work*, but *believes* on him who justifies the ungodly, his faith is credited for righteousness (Romans 4:5, emphasis added).**

Who is justified? Not the person who is partly trusting in Jesus and partly trusting in his works. No. It's the person who has *stopped working*—i.e., who no longer trusts his works but only believes in Jesus. You can believe in either Jesus or your works, but never both at once.

That was Paul's complaint against the false teachers who were adding circumcision to faith. They were telling people that salvation depended on believing in Jesus *and* getting circumcised. But Paul thundered that adding anything to faith turned it into a cursed gospel!

(Galatians 1:6-9). If the Galatians got circumcised, Christ would be of no benefit to them:

> **Take note! I, Paul, am telling you that if you get yourselves circumcised, Christ will not benefit you at all. Again I testify to every man who gets himself circumcised that he is obligated to do the entire law. You who are trying to be justified by the law are alienated from Christ; you have fallen from grace (Galatians 5:2-4).**

The Galatians were already justified, so this was an issue of Christian living: Christ would be of no benefit to them in their *sanctification*. From that I must conclude if an *unbeliever* partly depends on Christ and partly on his works for salvation, Christ will be of no benefit to him for his *justification*, i.e., he will not be saved at all. That was Israel's problem:

> **What should we say then? Gentiles, who did not pursue righteousness, have obtained righteousness—namely the righteousness that comes from faith. But Israel, pursuing the law of righteousness, has not achieved the righteousness of the law. Why is that? Because they did not pursue it by faith, but as if it were by works (Romans 9:30-32a).**

If you pursue salvation based on your works, you'll miss it. There is only one way to be saved: by faith in Jesus apart from works. Period. Any other option is cursed.

F. Conclusion

The Free Grace position clearly and unequivocally believes in salvation by *underserved grace*. God, in His mercy, saves ungodly people who have stopped trusting in themselves and who simply believe in Jesus for their salvation. Our works are excluded from the picture, but not the responsibility to believe.

Endnotes

1. J. I. Packer and O. R. Johnston, *Martin Luther on the Bondage of the Will* (N.P.: Fleming H. Revell, 1957), 59.
2. Packer, *Martin Luther*, 58.
3. Roger E. Olson, *Arminian Theology: Myths and Realities* (Downers Grove, IL: IVP Academic, 2006), 32.
4. Quoted in Roger E. Olson, "What Is An Arminian?" (blog)
5. Johannes P. Louw and Eugene Albert Nida, *Greek-English Lexicon of the New Testament: Based on Semantic Domains* (New York, NY: United Bible Societies, 1996), 298.
6. William Arndt et al., *A Greek-English Lexicon of the New Testament and Other Early Christian Literature* (Chicago, IL: University of Chicago Press, 2000), 1079.
7. John 1:12; 3:15-18, 36; 5:24; 6:35, 40, 47; 7:38; 8:24; 11:25-26; 20:31; Acts 2:21; 8:12-13, 37; 10:43; 11:17-18; 13:39; 15:7-9; 16:31; 18:8; Rom 1:16-17; 3:22, 25-28, 30; 4:3, 5, 9, 11, 13, 16-17, 18-22; 5:1-2; 9:30-33; 10:4, 6, 9-11, 14-17; 11:20-21. I could go on but I hope that establishes the point.
8. James Swanson, *Dictionary of Biblical Languages with Semantic Domains: Greek (New Testament)* (Oak Harbor: Logos Research Systems, Inc., 1997).
9. F. Arndt William and F. Wilbur Gingrich, *A Greek-English Lexicon of the New Testament and Other Early Christian Literature* (Chicago, IL: The University of Chicago Press, 1957), 816.
10. Louw and Nida, *Greek-English Lexicon,* 375.

5

Security of the Saints

What happens after you believe in Jesus? Are you safe? Are you guaranteed to grow in faith and good works? Is apostasy possible?

Calvinists teach the perseverance of the saints. That means God causes everyone He has predestined to salvation to persevere in faith and good works until death. As Boettner says:

> "All who were chosen by God, redeemed by Christ, and given faith by the Spirit are eternally saved. They are kept in faith by the power of the Almighty God and thus persevere to the end."[1]

Thus, if you fail to persevere to the end, that proves you were never saved (i.e., elect) to begin with.

Meanwhile, many Arminians believe that if you fail to cooperate with God's grace you can lose your salvation. In discussing the "means of grace" J. Kenneth Grider wrote:

> "in the understanding of this theological tradition, a believer may fall from grace. Taking steps to prevent this is therefore urgent...God's continued grace is needed if we are to maintain our redeemed status and if we are to live holy lives."[2]

For Arminians, you must maintain your redeemed status—your salvation—or risk losing it.

By contrast, the Free Grace position holds to eternal security, i.e., *once saved, always saved*. However, our understanding is not identical to the Calvinist doctrine of perseverance. Though the two have been used as synonyms, they shouldn't be, as I'll explain.

A. Believers Are Eternally Secure

Where is eternal security taught in Scripture? For one, the Lord Jesus taught it in His conversation with the woman at the well:

> **Jesus said, "Everyone who drinks from this water will get thirsty again. But whoever drinks from the water that I will give him *will never get thirsty again.* In fact, the water I will give him will become a well of water springing up in him for eternal life" (John 4:13-14, emphasis added).**

Since Jesus was resting by a well, the Lord naturally used it as an illustration for salvation, drawing a contrast between two types of water. After this woman drank the well water, she would become thirsty again. But one drink of His living water would mean she would never thirst again, and it would "spring up into everlasting life" (v 14). How does that prove eternal security? If Arminians are right that she could lose her salvation, then she could thirst again. But Jesus says that would never happen. One drink and she would get living water (i.e., the Holy Spirit), eternal life, and her thirst would be eternally satiated. I take that as an evocative picture of eternal security.

If Jesus' argument is too poetic, then consider what He promised in the next chapter:

> **"Truly I tell you, anyone who hears my word and believes him who sent me has eternal life and will not come under judgment but has passed from death to life" (John 5:24).**

There's no mistaking the imagery here. Everyone understood that salvation involved God's judgment. Jesus promised that everyone who believes in Him will *not* come into that judgment (John 5:24).[3] Why not? Because the moment you believe, Jesus gives you the verdict ahead of time—you've *already* passed from death to life. If you could lose your salvation, then Jesus should have said you *might* not come into judgment or you *hopefully won't* come under judgment, but there's no way to know for sure. Instead, He said you *will not*. It's guaranteed the moment you believe because believers are eternally secure.

To press the point, in the next chapter, Jesus made this promise:

> **"Everyone the Father gives me will come to me, and the one**

> **who comes to me *I will never cast out*" (John 6:37, emphasis added).**

This, to me, is one of the most comforting promises in Scripture. If you "come" to Jesus—another metaphor for believing in Him—He promises to never cast you out. Never. Once He has you, He won't let go. An Arminian says Jesus might cast you out depending on whether you maintain your redeemed status or not. But Jesus promises that will never happen. In other words, you're secure.

Later in the Gospel, the Lord made the point even clearer:

> **"I give them eternal life, and they will never perish. No one will snatch them out of my hand. My Father, who has given them to me, is greater than all. No one is able to snatch them out of the Father's hand" (John 10:28-29).**

I like to use this verse to explain eternal security to children. I'll clench a dollar in my fist and challenge a child (preferably a weak-looking one!) to take it from me. She'll struggle and try to pry my fingers apart and fail to do it. Then I'll clasp the dollar in both fists and ask her to try again. At that point, she'll give up because she knows if she can't take the dollar out of one hand, she certainly can't take it out of both. Salvation is like that. Once you're in Jesus' and the Father's hands by faith, no one can snatch you away. And since you're held securely, you can't jump out of the Father's hand any more than the dollar can jump out of my fist. The Father is "greater than all" including you, which means the believer is secure forever.

Eternal security is also taught elsewhere in Scripture.

B. Forgiveness Implies Security

Arminians who believe they can lose their salvation assume they can sin their salvation away. But if justification is true, that's impossible. Why? The blessing of justification includes the blessing of total forgiveness. They go together like two sides of the same coin. When Paul explained justification, he emphasized the forgiveness aspect:

> **Likewise, David also speaks of the blessing of the person to whom God credits righteousness apart from works:**
>
> **Blessed are those whose lawless acts are forgiven**
> **and whose sins are covered.**
> **Blessed is the person**
> **the Lord will never charge with sin (Romans 4:6-8).**

The blessing of justification includes being forgiven, having your sins covered, and being guaranteed that God will never charge you with them (cf. 2 Cor 5:19). That makes sense because it would be contradictory to consider someone perfectly righteous and guilty at the same time.

Christians have always understood that forgiveness is central to salvation. Jesus' very name refers to how He saves people from their sins (Matt 1:21; cf. John 1:29). When the risen Jesus commissioned the apostles, he sent them out with the good news of forgiveness:

> **Jesus said to them again, "Peace be with you. As the Father has sent me, I also send you." After saying this, he breathed on them and said, "Receive the Holy Spirit. *If you forgive the sins of any, they are forgiven them; if you retain the sins of any, they are retained*" (John 20:21-23, emphasis added).**

And so, when the apostles evangelized, they preached that judgment was coming, but people could be forgiven by believing in Jesus:

> **"He commanded us to preach to the people and to testify that he is the one appointed by God to be the judge of the living and the dead. All the prophets testify about him that *through his name everyone who believes in him receives forgiveness of sins*" (Acts 10:42-43, emphasis added).**

They proclaimed the good news of Christ's death and resurrection (Acts 13:27-31), and the forgiveness and justification available through faith in Him:

> **"For David, after serving God's purpose in his own generation, fell asleep, was buried with his fathers, and decayed, but the one God raised up did not decay. Therefore, let it be known to you, brothers and sisters, that *through this man forgiveness of sins is being proclaimed to you.* Everyone who *believes* is *justified* through him from everything that you could not be *justified* from through the law of Moses" (Acts 13:36-39, emphasis added).**

As Paul reminded the Colossians, when they believed in Jesus, they were made alive (i.e., regenerated) and forgiven of *all* sin:

> **And when you were dead in trespasses and in the uncircumcision of your flesh, he made you alive with him *and forgave us all our trespasses* (Colossians 2:13, emphasis added).**

Jesus' death accomplished what the animal sacrifices of the Old Testament never could—total forgiveness (cf. Hebrews 10:4; John 1:29).

Given the truth that believers are completely forgiven, can you see why you can't sin your salvation away? Any sin that might be grounds for you to lose your salvation has already been paid for. They were already imputed to Christ and forgiven you when you believed in Jesus, so they can't affect your eternal salvation.

Justification and forgiveness imply eternal security.

C. Sanctification Is Not Guaranteed

You may still be wondering how eternal security in Free Grace is different from the perseverance of the saints in Calvinism. If so, this next point should clarify things.

Unlike in Calvinism, Free Grace believes in eternal security *without the guarantee of perseverance*. Being sanctified and growing to spiritual maturity are not automatic. Someone can be eternally secure and fail to grow.

That is not the case according to Calvinism's doctrine of perseverance. In that view, the elect are caused to persevere. That is part of their belief in predestination and monergism, according to which God does all the work of salvation. The problem is, if sanctification is monergistic, you would expect Christians to be sinless, and we're clearly not. Instead, we all sin every day, and we're all at different levels of spiritual maturity. Why would that be if God is the sole cause of sanctification? The Calvinistic doctrine of perseverance isn't true to experience. But more importantly, it isn't true to Scripture.

According to the Free Grace view, eternal security neither guarantees nor depends upon our practical sanctification. People will grow spiritually at different rates, sometimes making progress and sometimes reverting to spiritual carnality. We're sanctified as we learn to walk by faith and abide in Christ, depending upon Him for every moment. But there's no guarantee that we will do that.

For example, when Paul wrote to the Corinthians, God evidently wasn't causing them to be sanctified. Indeed, Paul said he couldn't talk to them as spiritual people:

> **For my part, brothers and sisters, *I was not able to speak to you as spiritual people but as people of the flesh, as babies in Christ.* I gave you milk to drink, not solid food, since you were not yet ready for it. In fact, *you are still not ready,* because *you are still worldly.* For since there is envy and strife among**

> **you, are you not worldly and behaving like mere humans? For whenever someone says, "I belong to Paul," and another, "I belong to Apollos," are you not acting like mere humans? (1 Corinthians 3:1-4, emphasis added).**

Look at how Paul describes them—the Corinthians were fleshly, babyish, worldly, and behaving like mere humans. How is that possible? It's because sanctification is conditional. Clearly, believers can fail to mature and remain worldly.

The Hebrews provide another example of Christians who willfully failed to grow:

> **We have a great deal to say about this, and it is difficult to explain, *since you have become too lazy to understand.* Although by this time you ought to be teachers, you need someone to teach you the basic principles of God's revelation again. You need milk, not solid food. Now everyone who lives on milk is inexperienced with the message about righteousness, *because he is an infant.* But solid food is for the mature—for those whose senses have been trained to distinguish between good and evil (Hebrews 5:11-14, emphasis added).**

How does the author describe the Hebrews? As lazy, basic, and inexperienced. The Hebrews ought to have been teachers, but instead had to go back to drinking from the baby bottle. How embarrassing!

The point is an eternally secure believer is not guaranteed to grow, but can waste his life being spiritually lazy and childish.

But he can also do something even worse.

D. Believers Can Apostatize

According to Calvinists, someone who is truly elect can't apostatize and leave the faith. They think that's impossible due to monergism. By contrast, Free Grace theologians recognize (along with Arminians) that the New Testament is filled with warnings against apostasy:

> **Timothy, my son, I am giving you this instruction in keeping with the prophecies previously made about you, so that by recalling them you may fight the good fight, having faith and a good conscience, *which some have rejected and have shipwrecked the faith.* Among them are Hymenaeus and Alexander, whom I have delivered to Satan, so that they may be taught not to blaspheme (1 Timothy 1:18-20, emphasis added).**

Paul encouraged Timothy to press on and fight the good fight of faith because he didn't want him to be like those who "rejected and have shipwrecked the faith." Since you can't shipwreck a faith you never had Paul was referring to believers who later rejected Jesus. Apostasy is a real possibility, even for someone like Timothy.

To emphasize the point, Paul then named two Christians who did just that: Hymenaeus and Alexander. They were apostates whom Paul delivered to Satan. That probably means they came under church discipline. They were kicked out of the community and sent back into the world, i.e., Satan's domain.

Later in the letter, Paul gave another warning:

> **Timothy, guard what has been entrusted to you, avoiding irreverent and empty speech and contradictions from what is falsely called knowledge. By professing it, *some people have departed from the faith* (1 Timothy 6:20-21, emphasis added).**

False teaching can lead someone to leave the faith. Once again, you can't depart from a faith that you never had. Only believers can apostatize.

That possibility is taught consistently throughout the New Testament which warns us that Christians can "depart from the truth" (2 Timothy 2:17-19), "stray from the truth" (James 5:19), "draw back" (Hebrews 10:38-39), "deny the faith," become "worse than an unbeliever" (1 Timothy 5:8), and can "turn away to follow Satan" (1 Timothy 5:14-15). To repeat, you cannot depart from, stray away from, deny, or turn away from something you never had. Believers can apostatize.

The big question is: what's the consequence for doing that? How do you reconcile (1) the truth of eternal security and (2) the truth of the possibility of apostasy? Free Grace theologians have come to recognize that while unfaithful believers *can't* lose their salvation, they *can* lose a great many things short of salvation, beginning with eternal rewards.

E. Believers Can Lose Eternal Rewards

Have you ever heard of eternal rewards? While they may not be prominent in other traditions, they're important to Free Grace theology. We see a sharp distinction between salvation and rewards. Whereas salvation is given by faith apart from our works (Ephesians 2:8-9), look at the basis for giving out rewards:

> **"Look, I am coming soon, and *my reward* is with me to repay**

> **each person *according to his work*" (Revelation 22:12, emphasis added).**

Rewards are given on the basis of what you've done. Obedience matters. Yes, your works are utterly useless for earning eternal salvation, but they're still useful *for helping your neighbors.*

Think of it this way. God calls us to love our neighbors because life is hard and people need help. Our imperfect good works can still benefit the people around us. If you see a woman with a flat tire and you pull over to help her change it, you won't be earning a place in heaven, but you'll be genuinely helping her. God sees those types of relatively good works and chooses to reward them. One day, believers will appear before Jesus, not to be judged for their salvation, but to have their works evaluated for rewards:

> **For we must all appear before the judgment seat of Christ, so that each may be *repaid* for what he has done in the body, whether good or evil (2 Corinthians 5:10, emphasis added).**

Salvation is a *gift*, but rewards are *payment* based on what you've done.

When Jesus taught about rewards, He compared it to *laying up treasure in heaven* (Matthew 6:19-21). While Free Grace theologians disagree about the nature of these treasures, we agree they provide a real incentive to Christian living.

Every Christian is responsible for laying up treasure. Paul compared it to building a house:

> **For no one can lay any foundation other than what has been laid down. That foundation is Jesus Christ. If anyone builds on the foundation with gold, silver, costly stones, wood, hay, or straw, each one's work will become obvious. For the day will disclose it, because it will be revealed by fire; the fire will test the quality of each one's work. If anyone's work that he has built survives, he will receive a reward. If anyone's work is burned up, he will experience loss, but he himself will be saved—but only as through fire (1 Corinthians 3:11-15).**

Every believer is a builder. The only question is what kind of materials are you using? Living a prodigal life is like building a house out of wood, hay, or straw while being faithful is like building it out of precious materials. When the fires of judgment come through, the cheap materials will be burned away, leaving behind the treasure.

But it's possible that the fires will leave nothing left. Notice that Paul says it's possible for a Christian's life to consist entirely of wood, hay, or straw so that all his works burn up, leaving nothing to reward. Will that person lose his salvation? No. Paul is explicit: "If anyone's work is burned up, he will experience loss, *but he himself will be saved—but only as through fire.*" In other words, believers are eternally secure. You can lose rewards but not salvation. In that sense, the doctrine of rewards complements both the doctrines of eternal security and apostasy.

F. A Better Approach to Problem Passages

On that note, when you recognize the Biblical teaching about (1) eternal security, (2) conditional sanctification and apostasy, and (3) eternal rewards, you can better understand other warning passages. For example, what is Paul warning about in these two texts?

> **"Now the works of the flesh are obvious: sexual immorality, moral impurity, promiscuity, idolatry, sorcery, hatreds, strife, jealousy, outbursts of anger, selfish ambitions, dissensions, factions, envy, drunkenness, carousing, and anything similar. I am warning you about these things—as I warned you before—that those who practice such things *will not inherit the kingdom of God*" (Galatians 5:19-21, emphasis added).**

Similarly, Paul warned the carnal Corinthians:

> **Instead, you yourselves do wrong and cheat—and you do this to brothers and sisters! Don't you know that the unrighteous will not inherit God's kingdom? Do not be deceived: No sexually immoral people, idolaters, adulterers, or males who have sex with males, no thieves, greedy people, drunkards, verbally abusive people, or swindlers will *inherit God's kingdom* (1 Corinthians 6:8-10, emphasis added).**

Paul warned these believers that people who practiced the vices he mentions (including the Corinthians who were wronging and cheating each other) would not *inherit the kingdom of God*. What does that mean? I can't tell you how many times people think these passages mean sinful Christians "will not be *saved*" or "will not *go to heaven*." That's not what Paul says or means.

Inheritance is a reward concept. It's the heavenly treasure Jesus called us to lay up. An unfaithful believer will still be *in* the kingdom, but you can *enter* it without having an *inheritance* within it. The Christian attitude should be the one encouraged by Jesus and described by Peter, who counseled us to add virtues to our faith. Why should we do that? Because while salvation is by faith apart from works, if we add virtues to our faith, we're promised *a rich entrance* into the kingdom:

> **For in this way, entry into the eternal kingdom of our Lord and Savior Jesus Christ will be richly provided for you (2 Peter 1:11).**

When Peter says an entrance will be "richly provided," he's referring to the amount of heavenly treasure or inheritance that will be waiting in the kingdom for faithful believers. But if someone is lazy, unfaithful, or becomes apostate, they'll have a poor entrance, i.e., little or no treasure. But they'll still enter the kingdom because believers are eternally secure, and salvation is by faith apart from works.

G. Ruling with Christ

One of the most prestigious rewards is to rule with Christ in His kingdom. In Genesis 1:26-28, we read that God created man to rule over creation. That has always been God's purpose for us, and it will be realized in the Messianic kingdom.

For example, in Jesus' Parable of the Minas, a nobleman (representing Jesus) goes to a far country to receive a kingdom. Before he left, he gave his servants (representing believers) money to invest, charging them to "Do business till I come" (Luke 19:13). When the nobleman came back, he evaluated how the servants did. Look at how he rewarded them:

> **"The first came forward and said, 'Master, your mina has earned ten more minas.' 'Well done, good servant!' he told him. 'Because you have been faithful in a very small matter, *have authority over ten towns*'" (Luke 19:16-17, emphasis added).**

Naturally, kingdoms have cities, and the new king rewards his best servants with authority over them. However, as the parable continues, the nobleman finds that one of the servants did nothing with his investment money. He utterly wasted his opportunity:

> **"And another came and said, 'Master, here is your mina. I have kept it safe in a cloth because I was afraid of you since you're a harsh man: you collect what you didn't deposit and reap what you didn't sow.'**

> **"He told him, 'I will condemn you by what you have said, you evil servant! If you knew I was a harsh man, collecting what I didn't deposit and reaping what I didn't sow, why, then, didn't you put my money in the bank? And when I returned, I would have collected it with interest.' So he said to those standing there, 'Take the mina away from him and give it to the one who has ten minas'" (Luke 19:20-26).**

That servant didn't get to rule. He missed that privilege and even had his *mina* taken away, depicting the loss of other rewards for faithful service, not the loss of salvation.

The goal of "ruling with Christ" is a recurring theme in Jesus' ministry. He promised the apostles they would be rewarded by ruling over the twelve tribes of Israel (Matthew 19:28). That's why the mother of James and John asked Him to let her sons rule with Him at His right and left hand (Matthew 20:21). But Jesus made it clear that would depend on what they would do, i.e., "drinking the cup" that He would drink, which refers to suffering (Matthew 20:22-23).

Paul picked up on the idea that ruling with Christ requires faithfully following Him in a very famous yet commonly misunderstood passage:

> **This saying is trustworthy:**
> **For if we died with him,**
> **we will also live with him;**
> ***if we endure, we will also reign with him;***
> ***if we deny him, he will also deny us;***
> **if we are faithless, he remains faithful,**
> **for he cannot deny himself (2 Timothy 2:11-13, emphasis added).**

Too many people read those words and think that Paul is saying that Jesus will deny people *their salvation*, when Paul clearly refers to *reigning with Christ*. If we endure in the faith, we'll reign with Him. If not, then He'll deny us that reward. No cities for the unfaithful servants. But again, this is a rewards issue, not a salvation issue.

By the way, this passage is more proof that believers can apostatize (i.e., we can "deny him") and still be eternally secure (i.e., even if we are "faithless" to Jesus, the Lord remains "faithful" to us).

H. Other Examples of Rewards

Once you recognize that eternal rewards are a Biblical category, you'll more easily recognize them throughout Scripture. For example, in each of the letters that Jesus wrote to the churches in Revelation, He promised rewards to those who would overcome. These are "the right to eat from the tree of life" (Revelation 2:7), "the crown of life" (2:10), "some of the hidden manna" (2:17), "a white stone" inscribed with "a new name" (2:17), "authority over the nations" (2:26), "white clothes" and having your name acknowledged (3:5), becoming "pillar in the temple of my God" (3:12), and having "the name of my God and the name of the city of my God" written on you, and "the right to sit with me on my throne" (3:21). Notice that having authority over the nations or sitting on His throne are references to the reward of ruling with Christ.

While it's hard to know whether to take these rewards literally or figuratively (Revelation is a book of symbols after all), none of those things are offered on the basis of simple belief in Jesus, but instead depend on enduring, conquering, heeding the Lord's voice, and being faithful unto death. Since not all Christians do that, not all will receive these rewards, hence Jesus' warning.

Losing rewards isn't the only negative consequence of sin.

I. Other Negative Consequences of Sin

Scripture is filled with other things that an eternally secure believer can lose. Whereas losing rewards is an eternal consequence, you could say these other things are *earthly* consequences.

For example, if you break a nation's law, you can lose your freedom or your life (Romans 13:1-4). You can quench the Spirit (1 Thessalonians 5:19) and lose your joy (Psalms 51:12a; Galatians 5:22). If you commit adultery, you can lose your marriage (Matthew 19:8-9). If you're arrogant, hot-tempered, or an excessive drinker, you can be excluded from ministry (cf. Titus 1:5-9). And lastly, as with the Corinthians, Paul warned that believers could lose both their health and their lives because of sin (1 Corinthians 11:30).

On the one hand, being eternally secure doesn't exempt you from the negative earthly consequences of sin. On the other hand, losing those things is not equivalent to losing salvation, but they are still serious losses. An eternally secure person can make his life miserable.

J. Eternal Security and Free Will

Arminians sometimes object that eternal security and free will are incompatible. They say that if you're free to believe saved, you should also be free to reject your salvation. "Shouldn't freewill work both ways?"

That's a good question with a simple answer: *choices have consequences*. Once you make a choice for good or for ill, you're not free to take back the consequences of it.

For example, if you go skydiving, you can jump out of the plane. But once you're in freefall, can you rewind the clock or transport yourself back into the plane? No. You have to live with the consequences of jumping.

Likewise, freely believing in Jesus has permanent consequences, too—*but very good ones!* At the moment of faith, you were born again, justified, forgiven, reconciled, and adopted into God's family. You might regret that fact later (apostasy is possible!), but you can't take it back or undo God's saving work in you. Believing in Jesus changes you forever.

K. Assurance of Salvation

All of what I have said about the security of the believer impacts assurance of salvation.

As we have seen, Calvinists and Arminians both believe that salvation depends on continuing in faith and good works until death. While Calvinists think God causes the elect to do that, Arminians think people must freely cooperate with God's grace to maintain their salvation. How does that affect assurance? Since no one knows the future, no one knows if they'll persevere. And since they don't know that, they can't be assured of their salvation. They can *hope* to be saved, but can't be *sure*—not if they really think about it (which, frankly, most people don't do).

By contrast, on the Free Grace view, you can be sure of your salvation. In fact, you can't believe in Jesus for salvation without being sure.

Assurance can be put in the form of a simple syllogism, where the major premise is the saving message itself, and the minor premise is that you believe it. The conclusion naturally follows—

P1: Whoever believes in the Lord Jesus will be saved (cf. Acts 16:31).
P2: I believe in the Lord Jesus.
C: Therefore, I will be saved.

P1: Everyone who believes is justified through him (cf. Acts 13:39).

P2: I believe in Jesus.
C: Therefore, I am justified through Him.

P1: For God loved the world in this way: He gave his one and only Son, so that everyone who believes in him will not perish but have eternal life (cf. John 3:16).
P1: I believe in God's one and only Son.
C: Therefore, I will not perish but have eternal life.

If you understand the good news about salvation and are persuaded that it's true, then you can't help but believe the conclusion and so be assured of your salvation. Believing the conclusion is what assurance means. Moreover, you'll remain assured *so long as you keep believing*. However, if you stop believing, you'll also stop being assured. You'll still be *saved*—because salvation doesn't depend on persevering in assurance—but you won't *enjoy* the salvation that you permanently have in Christ.

L. Conclusion

Free Grace theology believes in the eternal security of the saints without the guarantee of persevering in the faith or of growing spiritually. On the contrary, we hold that believers can fail to mature, or even apostatize. But doing that will not result in a loss of salvation, but in a loss of rewards and earthly blessings.

Endnotes

1. Lorraine Boettner, *The Reformed Faith* (Phillipsburg, NJ: Presbyterian and Reformed Publishing Company, 1983), 27-28.
2. J. Kenneth Grider, *A Wesleyan-Holiness Theology* (Kansas City, MO: Beacon Hill Press, 1994), 511.
3. Paul makes the same argument. The believer who is justified is guaranteed to be saved from the last judgment (cf. Rom 1:16-18; 2:5-11; 5:9; Rev 20:11-15).

Conclusion

There you have the case for the Free Grace position. If you've been considering Calvinism's case for TULIP, or Arminianism's case for ROSES, I hope you see that Free Grace's LOTUS is a legitimate third option, if not the most faithful Biblical one.

To summarize—

First, we believe in *liable depravity*, where sin affects every aspect of our being without robbing us of the ability and responsibility to believe.

Second, we believe in *occupational election*, where God chooses people, places, and things to serve His purposes.

Third, we believe in a *tiered atonement*, where the cross has different benefits for different people, given under different conditions.

Fourth, against all forms of works salvation we believe in salvation by *underserved grace*, where believing in Jesus is the one and only condition to be saved.

Fifth, and finally, we believe in *the security of the saints*, where salvation can never be lost under any circumstances, but eternal rewards and other benefits can be.

If you're reading this on a bus ride home, in a coffee shop, or in a quiet corner of a library, you might be feeling overwhelmed. I did! When I first began studying these issues, the questions were so big, and I knew so little about theology, that I doubted whether I would ever figure it all out. I want you to know that learning theology well takes time. It's no different than learning a language or a new skill—

you don't become good at it overnight. It takes years of practice. So give yourself time, grace, and space to learn, and show the same grace to others! Always remember everyone's learning journey is different.

Most of all, trust Jesus. Salvation depends on simple faith in Him, not on becoming a theologian.

For Further Study

If you would like to explore Free Grace theology in greater depth, or if you would like to see our other materials please visit:

Free Grace International
www.freegrace.in

You can also contact me with your questions at shawn@freegrace.in, or find me on social media.

To study Free Grace theology more, I recommend starting with these books (remembering there is variety within Free Grace).

A. Introductions

Bing, Charles C. *Simply by Grace: An Introduction to God's Life-Changing Gift* (Grand Rapids, MI: Kregel, 2009).

Evans, Tony. *The Tony Evans Study Bible* (Nashville, TN: Holman, 2019).

Hodges, Zane C. *Absolutely Free! A Biblical Reply to Lordship Salvation* (Grand Rapids, MI: Zondervan, 1989).

Kitchen, Lucas. *Eternal Life: Believe to Be Alive* (Longview, TX: Free Grace International, 2021).

Wilkin, Robert N. *Confident in Christ: Living By Faith Really Works* (Irving, TX: Grace Evangelical Society, 1999).

B. Answers to Problem Passages

The Grace New Testament Commentary, Revised Edition, ed. Robert N. Wilkin (Denton, TX: Grace Evangelical Society, 2019).

21 Tough Questions about Grace, ed. Grant Hawley (Allen, TX: Bold Grace, 2015).

Bing, Charles C. *Grace, Salvation & Discipleship: How to Understand Some Difficult Biblical Passages* (N.P.: Grace Theology Press, 2015).

Rokser, Dennis M. *Shall Never Perish Forever: Is Salvation Forever or Can It Be Lost?* (Duluth, MN: Grace Gospel Press, 2012).

C. Other Studies

Freely By His Grace: Classical Free Grace Theology, eds. J. B. Hixon, Rick Whitmire, and Roy B. Zuck (Duluth, MN: Grace Gospel Press, 2012).

Anderson, David R. *Free Grace Soteriology*, Revised Edition (N.P.: Grace Theology Press, 2012).

Dillow, Joseph. *Final Destiny: The Future Reign of The Servant Kings* (N.P.: Grace Theology Press, 2018).

Eaton, Michael A. *No Condemnation: A Theology of Assurance of Salvation* (Carlisle: Piquant Editions, 2011).

Hodges, Zane C. *The Epistle of James: Proven Character Through Testing* (Corinth, TX: Grace Evangelical Society, 2015).

Kerrey, Robert J. *How Does God Draw People to Believe in Jesus?: A Biblical Analysis of Alternatives and Why It Matters* (N.P.: Grace Theology Press, 2019).

Lazar, Shawn. *Chosen to Serve: Why Divine Election Is to Service, Not to Eternal Life* (Denton, TX: Grace Evangelical Society, 2017).

Thieme Jr., R. B. *Reversionism* (Houston, TX: R. B. Thieme Jr. Bible Ministries, 1972, 2000).

D. Websites

www.facebook.com/groups/freegracetheologydiscussiongroup
www.freegrace.in
www.faithalone.org
www.freegraceallliance.com
www.gracelife.org
www.c4capologetics.com
www.misthology.org
www.redeeminggod.com

Scripture Index

Old Testament

New Testament

Subject Index

SHAWN LAZAR (BTh, McGill; MA, Free University, Amsterdam) was born and raised in Montreal, Canada. He and his wife Abby live with their three children in Denton, TX. He writes and edits for Free Grace International (www.freegrace.in). Listen to his podcast, *Chapter by Chapter with Shawn Lazar* on all the most popular platforms. His other books include:

- *Beyond Doubt: How to Be Sure of Your Salvation*
- *Chosen to Serve: Why Divine Election Is to Service, Not to Eternal Life'*
- *One-Point Preaching: A Law and Gospel Model*
- *Scripturalism and the Senses: Reviving Gordon H. Clark's Apologetic*
- *It Takes God to Be a Man: The Spiritual Theology of Major Ian Thomas*
- *Free Grace Family Catechism*

Made in the USA
Columbia, SC
02 April 2025